D1745525

THE UNQUENCHABLE LIGHT

270
L359u

THE UNQUENCHABLE LIGHT

Kenneth Scott Latourette

D. Willis James Professor of Missions and Oriental History in Yale University

The William Belden Noble Lectures
in Harvard University, for 1940

THE RELIGIOUS BOOK CLUB
121, CHARING CROSS ROAD
LONDON, W.C.2

995

This Edition . . . 1945

BRITISH ISLES NAZARENE COLLEGE LIBRARY

WITHDRAWN

PRINTED IN GREAT BRITAIN
BY JARROLD AND SONS LTD., NORWICH

CONTENTS

Since the lectures which constitute this little book were delivered, events in the world at large have been moving with great rapidity. We have seen Pearl Harbour and the Japanese occupation of the Philippines, the East Indies, numbers of the other islands in the Pacific, and much of the mainland of South-east Asia. There has been the march of the German armies eastward, followed by their retreat under the amazing resurgence of Russia. None of these events, spectacular though they have been, have altered in any substantial fashion the conclusions set forth in this book. To be sure, large areas in which the younger churches have been planted are now cut off by Japanese arms from the founding older churches. The devastation of Europe, the traditional stronghold of much of Western Christianity, has proceeded apace. Yet if anything the picture is brighter for Christianity than it was three years ago. Such fragmentary news as has reached us from behind the wall of the Japanese armed forces indicates that the younger churches have to an amazing degree displayed inner vitality. There have been losses, both in morale and in numbers. That was to be expected. But there has been a persistence of the Christian faith, often accompanied with great heroism. In Europe we have seen the recognition by the Russian Government of the vitality of the Russian Orthodox Church, and a recession of the prolonged anti-Christian campaign in that vast land. We have also witnessed the resistance which the churches in German-occupied lands have presented to the invader, a resistance which has not only preserved the life of these churches, but which has also protested against the atrocities inflicted upon the Jews, a people largely of another faith. Organizationally Christianity in Europe may have been weakened by the events of the past few years. In vigour it has displayed a strength quite unsuspected by its enemies or its despondent friends. As the gloom has deepened in great areas of the world, the light has more and more proved to be unquenchable.

KENNETH SCOTT LATOURETTE

YALE UNIVERSITY,
      December 1943

PREFATORY STATEMENT
THE WILLIAM BELDEN NOBLE LECTURES

Terms proposed by the Founder and accepted by the President and Fellows of Harvard College, November 26, 1906

"The foundation having been established in memory of William Belden Noble shall bear his name and be known as The William Belden Noble Lectures. . . .

"The object of the Founder of the Lectures is to continue the mission of her husband, whose supreme desire was to extend the influence of Jesus as 'the Way, the Truth, and the Life,' and to illustrate and enforce the words of Jesus— 'I am come that they might have life and that they might have it more abundantly.' The Founder has in view the presentation of the personality of Jesus, as given in the New Testament, or unfolded in the history of the Christian Church, or illustrated in the inward experience of His followers, or as the inspiration to Christian Missions for the conversion of the world. Both the Founder and he in whose name the lectures are established were in deep sympathy with the teaching of the late Phillips Brooks. . . . It is the desire of the Founder that the Lecturer for each year shall be himself animated by the further motive which inspires this foundation—the hope of arousing in young men, and primarily in the students of Harvard University, the joy of service for Christ and humanity, especially in the ministry of the Christian Church. The scope of the Lectures is believed to be as wide as the highest interests of humanity. With this end in view—the perfection of the spiritual man, and the consecration, by the spirit of Jesus, of every department of human character, thought, or activity—the Lecturer will choose his subject. . . .

"Each printed copy of the Lectures in each and every year shall contain a prefatory statement of the origin of this foundation and its purpose in the mind of the Founder as given above. . . . The title-page and the outer cover of each printed copy shall bear the name of the foundation as well as the special title for the year, the date of delivery, and the Lecturer's name."

AUTHOR'S ACKNOWLEDGMENT

The author wishes at the outset to express his thanks to Harvard University. It was its invitation to deliver the William Belden Noble lectures which was the occasion and the incentive for this book. The unfailing hospitality and courtesy of the officers and faculty, and especially of Dean Willard L. Sperry of the Divinity School and Professor Crane Brinton, Chairman of the Department of History, helped to make the semester of weekly pilgrimages from New Haven to Cambridge which preceded and accompanied the lectures a pleasure rather than a burden. The author, too, is deeply indebted to Mrs. Charles T. Lincoln for typing the manuscript and for helpful suggestions as to literary style. To the many others, colleagues and students, too numerous to catalogue, but each making a contribution by the stimulus of fresh and keen insight, the author would in this collective fashion make grateful acknowledgment.

INTRODUCTION

No fact of history is more amazing than the spread of the influence of Jesus. Jesus sprang from humble surroundings among a subject people who were unimportant politically. His public career was short. At most it was only about three years and it may have been as brief as a year and a half. He wrote no book. He left behind Him no carefully systematized body of teachings. Usually He spoke as occasion offered, adapting His message to the transient situation and the changing audience. He seems to have taken little or no thought for a continuing organization to perpetuate His work. His death appeared not so much tragic as pitiful and futile. On that first Good Friday night it is doubtful whether any thoughtful observer, even if he had been sympathetic, would have forecast a prolonged life for the influence of Jesus. He would probably have predicted that this Galilean would be promptly forgotten and would be simply another of those unremembered idealists who, to their own sorrow, have pitted their feeble strength against entrenched interests and have perished.

Yet no other life ever lived on this planet has been so potent in the affairs of men. The most widely spread of the religions of mankind, Christianity, has Jesus as its central figure. Christianity is not solely the product of Jesus. Into it various other components have entered. Nor has Christianity been uniform. It has varied from age to age, from country to country, and even from individual to individual. Yet all the many forms which Christianity has taken have honoured Jesus. To a greater or less extent His influence has been present in each of them. From Jesus, through Christianity, have issued impulses which have helped to shape every phase of civilization. His influence has grown with the passing of the years and has never been so powerful as in the past century and a quarter. Its course has been like that of the incoming tide. Like the tide it has moved forward in waves. Each major wave has been followed by a major recession. But each major wave has set a new high-water mark and each major recession has been less pronounced than its predecessor.

In an earlier book, "Anno Domini," the author has attempted to sketch the course of this influence and has sought to set forth what seems to him to be its significance for history and what it appears to him to disclose of the meaning of the universe in which man finds himself and of the fashion in which the universe deals with man. The yardsticks employed for measuring the advance and the recession were, first, geographic spread, second, the number and the strength of the new movements whose origin can be traced to Jesus, and, third, the effect of Jesus upon individual lives and upon various aspects of civilization. The first two are, in their main outlines, fairly easily determined. When tested by them, the pattern of advance seems incontestable. The impact upon individuals and upon civilization is not so readily measured. This is partly because of the repeated difficulty of discovering beyond the possibility of cavil the presence of the influence of Jesus. It is also partly because, even when the fact of that presence has been established, the precise part which it has had is not quickly ascertained. Yet, after allowances for all these qualifications have been made, the increase in the influence of Jesus seems clear and the rough accuracy of the simile appears, at least to the present author, to be indubitable.

A further question immediately emerges which was not dealt with in "Anno Domini." By what processes has the influence of Jesus spread? By what means did an impulse, at the outset so unsystematized and even inchoate, perpetuate itself and grow? How was it that ideas and ideals so contradictory to much in human nature and alien to all of the cultures in which they gained currency attained such wide power?

We wish to know, moreover, why this influence persisted and increased in some areas and not in others. In some regions and among some peoples it long failed to gain entrance and then, when it obtained admittance, did not flourish. In others where it gave promise of an important future it disappeared. In still others where it was once potent it dwindled. Why this uneven record?

Why, moreover, has the influence of Jesus gone forward by great pulsation, and why has each major advance been followed by a recession? What accounts for each of the forward-moving waves and for each ebb? Are these fortuitous or does a common pattern run through them all?

It is clear that the influence of Jesus does not progress simply through the spontaneous response of the innate goodness of men. Man is not by nature either fully good or completely rational. There is that in some men which at once welcomes Jesus and His message. There is that in others which is roused to furious opposition. Still more never understand Him. It was thus in the days of His flesh. Some few held to Him. Others crucified Him. Still more were swayed by the opinions of the tough-minded and strong-willed about them and never really comprehended either the loyalty or the opposition. So it has been through the centuries. The responses to Jesus have varied. They have been determined not simply by the quality of Jesus or by the representations of Him made by His professed followers, although these have entered into the issue, but also by other factors, some of them quite remote from Jesus and His teachings.

Still another question concerns us. What of the future? Mankind has just passed through a period in which the influence of Jesus has been more widespread and has done more to shape the human race as a whole than at any previous time. From the standpoint of that influence the hundred years between 1815 and 1914 were the great century. We have now entered a new age. The familiar features of the nineteenth century are being rapidly left behind. The movements and forces in connection with which the influence of Jesus spread, and many of which were to a large extent the fruits of that influence, are weakening, disappearing, or being modified almost past recognition. Are we witnessing another major recession? If so, is the previous pattern to persist, and will the recession be less pronounced than its predecessors? Or is the pattern to be broken and has a recession begun which will be more profound than any before it? Is the influence of Jesus on its way out? What are the forces with which it must reckon? How likely are these to permit it to endure? If it does survive, what forms is it likely to assume? All of this must partake of prophecy. Prophecies are notoriously fallible: "whether there be prophecies they shall fail." Yet something within us urges us to attempt to see into the future. We must, moreover, plan. We must act. We must set our course by such stars as we can see, always prepared to change it as new currents, shoals, rocks, and channels are disclosed in the uncharted seas into which we sail. We must, then, attempt to look ahead. The study of the past to which the major portion of this book is devoted should give us some clue to the probable course as yet untraversed. A knowledge of the forces which have made for the advance and the recession of the Christian tide should enable us to assess the probabilities for the age before us. If we can discover what combinations have previously accounted for gains in the influence of Jesus and what have militated against that influence and then can compare them with what we see happening in the world of to-day, we should have a basis for forecasting with some degree of accuracy the main trends in at least the present and the coming generation.

In our survey our chronology is fairly well determined by the waves of the incoming Christian tide and by the major ebbings. First is a period which covers approximately five centuries to A.D. 500. In it the Christian faith took form and the overwhelming majority of the population of the Roman Empire were won to at least a formal allegiance. Christianity became largely identified with the Roman Empire. There followed, in the second place, a prolonged and disheartening recession. This was approximately four and a half centuries in length. In it some gains were made and, actually, Christian communities became scattered over a wider area than they had been in A.D. 500. Yet in the Mediterranean basin the solid Christian bloc was broken. In about half the former Græco-Roman world Christians became minorities on the defensive. The Roman Empire, which had seemed the great bulwark of Christianity, itself dwindled and in the West largely collapsed. Barbarians, mostly pagans, poured in from the East and the North and dealt blow after blow to Christianity in Europe. The Arabs, bearers of a new faith, swept in from the south-east and made the Crescent dominant over fully half the coast of the Mediterranean. The morale of Christians and of the Church ebbed sickeningly. A third period stretched from about A.D. 950 to about A.D. 1350. In it the wave again moved forward. Christianity, and with it the influence of Jesus, spread more widely and in at least one major area had a more profound effect upon culture than ever before. Then followed, as the fourth period, the second major recession. Christianity again lost ground and the morale of Christians waned, although not so markedly as in the four and a half centuries after A.D. 500. Not so long a period elapsed until the next great forward movement. The decline continued only from about A.D. 1350 to about A.D. 1500. The fifth period was the third advance, from about A.D. 1500 to about the middle of the eighteenth century. In it the influence of Jesus again established a new record for geographic extent, gave birth to an unprecedented number of new movements, and had profound effects upon human culture. A brief recession followed, as the sixth period, from about the middle of the eighteenth century until A.D. 1815. The loss of territory and the shrinkage of morale within the Christian community were much less pronounced than in the preceding two recessions. Indeed, in some quarters fresh gains had begun even before the recession had become obvious. The fourth great advance, and the seventh period, was roughly from A.D. 1815 to A.D. 1914. From the standpoint of geographic extent, new movements of marked vitality, and effects upon civilization the world around, this was, as we have suggested, the greatest century which the influence of Jesus has thus far known. It has been followed, in the eighth place, from A.D. 1914 to a date still in the future, by a period which, because we have only begun to enter it, is hard to characterize. In some of its aspects, especially in the past six or seven years, it is another recession. Yet in others of its features it has witnessed phenomenal gains. If, after attempting to strike an average, advance is seen to have been registered, it is clear that it is not so marked as in the hundred years before A.D. 1914. Some are inclined to believe that the forward movements since A.D. 1914 have been chiefly the final surges of the wave which was so strong in the nineteenth century. That analysis, however, is too simple. It fails to take account of the flooding tide of which waves and recessions seem only to have been the superficial features.

To this story we must now turn. We are here, we must again remind ourselves, to be concerned primarily with the processes by which the influence of Jesus has spread and the reasons for its gains and for its ebb or disappearance in some periods and areas. We have here only incidentally to do with the effects of that influence and of the details of the spread. Our purpose, too, is to gain insight into the present and future, from our knowledge of the previous course to obtain perspective on the bewildering changes about us and, if possible, to win some inkling of the course ahead.

In this survey we are to see again and again the partial dependence of the influence of Jesus upon forces extraneous to it. Some of these, indeed, have been contradictory to it and have done violence to its essence. We shall see the influence of Jesus balked in huge areas. While we shall hint at its profound effects upon culture after culture, we shall need to remind ourselves that no culture has fully embodied the ethics of Jesus. Always a tension has existed between the Christian ideal and actual human society. In the sense of being even approximately conformed to Jesus, for no section of mankind has the word Christian or Christendom ever been an accurate appellation.

Yet the spread and persistence of the influence of Jesus can never be ascribed primarily to external circumstances. Always the essential factor has been an inner vitality. No matter by what other forces the spread of Christianity has been facilitated, and these have been varied and many, most of the active agents have been those caught by Jesus and dedicated to Him. Never have they perfectly embodied him. The greatest of them have been aware of falling short of "the high calling of God in Christ Jesus." Some have been palpably imperfect and unworthy. Yet common to all the spread of Christianity has been the compelling attraction of Jesus. He has been the persistent and the enduring light. That light has had to contend with darkness. Sometimes the two have seemed to be mixed. In places the light has been quenched. Yet always somewhere it has continued to shine. When human history is seen in the long perspective of the centuries the path of the light has broadened. It has been shining more and more—even though the perfect day seems still very remote.

This is primarily an essay. It has eschewed the outward and visible paraphernalia of scholarship. It has deliberately denied itself footnotes and appended bibliographies. For those desiring these adjuncts to scholarship, the author's "History of the Expansion of Christianity," now in process of appearing, is available. It is upon facts elaborately documented in those volumes that the following chapters are based. This little book is, however, no mere culling from the larger work. It is an attempt at a fresh interpretation of one phase of the story there narrated. It is hoped that many will find it of aid in understanding what some of us are convinced is the central current of human history, at once the clue and the hope of the human drama.

KENNETH SCOTT LATOURETTE

YALE UNIVERSITY

CHAPTER I: THE INITIAL ADVANCE

~~~~~~

The wonder of the winning of the Roman Empire to the Christian faith has never ceased to engage the interest of the historian and to lure him to search for its causes.

Christianity began with one whose public career was so short, whose teachings were seemingly so casual and so conditioned by a particular view of history, and whose death was apparently due to such impractical idealism, that some scholars have held His connection with it to have been only a minor, even though possibly an essential, cause of its existence. They have sought elsewhere, albeit without convincing results, the secret of its vitality and its appeal.

At the outset Christianity was, to all surface appearances, simply one of several sects of Judaism. In the Roman Empire it had to make its way against the competition of many other religions and cults, numbers of which were long established and were an integral part of the dominant culture. It met the opposition of the state, an opposition which from time to time flared up in severe, general persecutions. Large numbers of the populace regarded Christianity with abhorrence and believed its adherents to be atheists, immoral, and enemies of the public welfare. Some of the educated despised Christianity for what they deemed its intellectual absurdities.

In spite of obstacles Christianity won. By A.D. 500 it was the professed faith of the vast majority within the Roman Empire. At that time that Empire, although it had suffered serious reverses, was still the most powerful state on the globe and embraced the strongest and most populous centre of civilization. Christianity, therefore, and with it the influence of Jesus, had made an impress upon a strategic area from which it might most readily spread to the rest of mankind. Changes, some of them revolutionary, had been wrought in Græco-Roman culture, although that culture was not so profoundly moulded by Christianity as some others were later to be. Most of the religions which had contested with Christianity the possession of the Mediterranean world had either been swept aside or had been

reduced to such weakness that they were no longer seriously
to be reckoned with. A rich and voluminous literature had
been produced. The Christian Church had been brought
into existence and had become, next to the state, the
strongest institution in the Empire. Christian theology had
made its appearance. Under the influence of Christianity
new forms of art and architecture were in process of
development. Christianity had contributed to the weakening of slavery and to the decline of some of the public
amusements, notably the sports of the arena, which were
at variance with the spirit of Jesus. Laws had been slightly
modified. Moreover, Christianity had begun to make its
way beyond the borders of the Roman Empire. In the
West it had been carried into Ireland and possibly beyond
the Roman wall into the north of Britain. In the East it
had gained a footing in the Persian Empire, in India, and
in Southern Arabia, and in the south of Ethiopia.

The processes by which this amazing spread was accomplished and the reasons for this triumph were complex.

Obviously the Roman Empire was a major factor. To
be sure, during much of the first three centuries the Roman
state was either passively or actively hostile. Yet it is one
of the commonplaces of history that the Roman Empire
afforded Christianity the opportunity which permitted the
Christian faith to acquire the outstanding position which
has been partly responsible for its expansion from that time
to this. It proved highly fortunate for the spread of His
influence that Jesus was born in the reign of the first Roman
Emperor. Had He been born a hundred years earlier, when
the wars which preceded the creation of the principate by
Augustus were still to be fought, or had He appeared two
centuries later when the imperial structure was beginning
to crumble, the course of the Christian faith would have
been much more difficult.

The fashion in which the Roman Empire was of assistance
in the spread of Christianity is so well known that it needs
here only the briefest mention. The *Pax Romana*, which
was established under Augustus and which for about two
centuries, with the exception of some severe, localized
rebellions, banished war to the borders of the realm, was

of great advantage to the expansion of a faith whose spirit flourishes best in time of peace. It was along the trade routes of the commerce encouraged by the *Pax Romana* that Christianity moved with a rapidity which never ceases to amaze us. Christianity placed its stamp upon Græco-Roman culture. That culture was the property of more millions than up to that time had ever been brought under one pattern of civilization. By becoming the religion of that culture, Christianity acquired an enormous advantage over its rivals for the allegiance of mankind. Beginning with Constantine, with the exception of the brief interlude of Julian, the Roman state espoused Christianity. Eventually it gave to that faith a preferred position over all its rivals.

We must note that after Christianity became the state cult, very little persecution was employed against its rivals. The Emperors gave it their support. Some of them encouraged and even commanded efforts to propagate it. Yet actual personal violence was seldom invoked against the adherents of pagan cults to induce the acceptance of Christianity. The use of force on a large scale to spread the faith was to wait until a later period.

The adoption of the Christian religion by the state did not insure the persistence of the influence of Jesus. Indeed, in some respects it was a greater menace than the earlier policy of persecution. A state cult is so bound to the government and under such constraint to support the secular authorities and their programmes that it finds difficulty in criticizing or judging the state. An official cult is supposed to give the powerful undergirding of religion to the existing régime. That had been a function of the pre-Christian official cults. In supplanting them, Christianity was expected to fill their role, only more effectively. This proved a serious handicap, as we are to see in later chapters. It partly accounts for the fate of Christianity in Russia in our day. In the area in which this subservience of the Church to the Roman state continued, Jesus had much less effect than in some regions where, because of the weakening or disappearance of that state, the Church obtained greater liberty.

The formation of the Roman Empire was both preceded and accompanied by another factor which facilitated the spread of Christianity—the disintegration of existing cultures. This disintegration had begun as early as Alexander. It was furthered by the cosmopolitan outlook and the impact of culture upon culture which followed the campaigns of Alexander and the more enduring conquests of Rome. The basin of the Mediterranean was being welded into a unit. As part of this process older cultures interpenetrated one another and were weakened. Countless individuals were cast adrift from their hereditary moorings and groups and were hungry for a faith which would give meaning to life. In many, a dissatisfaction arose with the current disintegration of morals and with the ethical standards of some of the older cults. The puerilities of the mythologies of Greek and Roman polytheism could only be partly met by the allegorizing employed by their defenders. Neither mind nor conscience was quite satisfied with them. Christian apologists must have found many responsive hearts when they rang the changes on the moral weaknesses of the gods. In the first centuries of the Roman Empire society was comparatively fluid and a new faith which could meet the demands of men could gain a hearing. Religiously the old foundations were being broken up and men were more open-minded and receptive than they had been for many generations—perhaps ever.

The close association which Christianity early established with Hellenism also proved of advantage in the spread of the faith. From a very early date—how early is a matter of debate—Greek was the major language of Christianity and continued to be such through most of the period. Christian thinkers were influenced by Greek philosophy. Some of them, indeed, were expert in it. Greek language and thought had wide circulation in the Roman Empire and the fact that Christianity came in Greek dress was of incalculable assistance to it.

On the other hand, the affiliation with Hellenism was not an unmixed benefit. There was danger that accommodation would go so far that the distinctive features of Jesus would be lost. In the wide portions of the Christian stream known as Gnosticism this tendency was very marked. What became the Church of the majority of Christians disavowed Gnosticism. There are those, however, who declare that even this majority church succumbed, although less spectacularly, to the trend, and that the dominant form of Christianity became a mystery cult in which Jesus was so distorted or forgotten that He had little effect. That extreme view, although brilliantly argued by able scholars, has not found acceptance with the majority of experts. The Jesus whom men knew in Galilee and Judea was cherished in the churches through which flowed the continuing Christian stream. He was interpreted in ways which partly obscured Him—as all interpretations must— but the most authentic records of His teachings, life, death, and resurrection were preserved and honoured, and He was given chief place in the Church which was declared to be His body.

The alliance of Christianity with the Roman Empire and with Hellenism, while of advantage in the Mediterranean world of the first five centuries, was a decided handicap to the eastward expansion of the faith.

Immediately to the east was the Persian Empire. When Christianity first became dominant in the Mediterranean Basin the Roman and Persian Empires were deadly rivals. Since Christianity was becoming identified with the Roman Empire, the rulers of Persia suspected such Christians as were in their realms of loyalty to Rome and of either actual or potential treason. This antipathy was accentuated by the inclination of at least some of the Christian Roman Emperors to take their fellow believers in Persia under their protection. That was notably the policy of Constantine. In the fifth century a national church was formed in Persia independent of the churches of the Roman Empire. It adopted the theology of Nestorius, which was anathema to the Roman state and its church. This must have helped to allay Persian suspicion. Yet Nestorianism was never able to overcome the initial prejudice against Christianity, and the fact that it was regarded as heretical by the majority of the Roman Empire cut it off from the fellowship of the strongest of the churches. Nestorianism made progress and planted extensive outposts in Central and Eastern Asia. However, only a little over two centuries after it had achieved a national organization in Persia it was forced to face Islam.

Christianity's close association with Hellenism, while of undoubted advantage in the Græco-Roman world, was probably a handicap in the East. Here by the third century the Hellenism which came in the wake of Alexander, while, as Buddhist art testifies, still potent, was a waning force. It was by no means as prominent as in the Roman Empire. It was probably in connection with commerce from the Mediterranean that Christianity was planted in Southern Arabia and Ethiopia. Yet most of such extension as Christianity enjoyed in India and in Central and Eastern Asia down into the fourteenth century was through Nestorianism and not through the churches of the Mediterranean world. Except for Nestorianism, and, to a less extent, Monophysitism, which was also at outs with the Roman state, east of Mesopotamia and to a certain extent in Mesopotamia Christianity remained semi-alien. Even Nestorianism and Monophysitism arose, so far as they were doctrinal, out of the controversies which had a Greek tinge and which were intensified by racial and political conditions in the Eastern Mediterranean. They were, accordingly, exotic to environments which did not have that background. The ecclesiastical language of Nestorians was Syriac, a tongue of the Eastern Mediterranean.

Christianity is basically so revolutionary that it is never fully at home anywhere. However, largely because of its association with Rome and with Hellenism, it did not become as firmly rooted east of Mesopotamia as in the Græco-Roman world.

In some areas within the Roman Empire the association with Hellenism and with Rome seems to have been a handicap. Christianity early established powerful strongholds in the Hellenistic cities of Syria, notably in that outstanding centre of Hellenism, Antioch. Yet much of Syria was but slightly touched by Hellenism. In the non-Hellenistic portions of Syria, Christianity was slow in making headway and was late in being accorded even nominal allegiance.

In North Africa the Berber elements of the population were never thoroughly won to a faith which was primarily the religion of the Roman overlords and of the Latinized and, later, Hellenized ruling classes. This was eventually to prove fatal.

When we have said that three of the factors contributing to the expansion of Christianity and with it to the spread of the influence of Jesus were the Roman Empire, the disintegration of old religious beliefs accompanied by a hunger for a morally and intellectually satisfying faith, and association with Hellenism, we have by no means accounted fully for the phenomenal growth of Christianity in its first five centuries. In the Roman Empire and in Hellenism the new faith encountered numerous rivals. Several of these had marked advantages over Christianity. Some were supported by the state and some were integral parts of Hellenism. Others did not set themselves as uncompromisingly against certain features of current life as did Christianity. We must seek further for the reasons for the victory of Christianity over its rivals in the Græco-Roman world.

The most active agent in the propagation of Christianity was the Church. Whether Jesus had planned the Church is a matter of debate. So far as our records of His sayings afford us evidence, He gave little if any thought to it. We certainly have no proof that He envisioned any such organization as had come into being by the close of the fifth century. At the outset the Christian fellowship took more than one form. It was not until about a century after Jesus that Christians began to regard as normal an ecclesiastical structure which had bishops as its chief administrative officers. Yet the Church, as continuing organized companies of Christians, was the chief means by which the influence of Jesus spread. This was true of the first five centuries. It has been true ever since.

The Church is a unique creation of Christianity. Whether or not Jesus planned it, it was His influence which brought it into being and it has always had Him as the centre of its professed loyalty. Into it entered many elements. It regarded itself as a continuation of the Jewish

community, as the true heir of Israel. To its early ritual
and organization the Jewish synagogue made important
contributions. Yet it was far more than a continuation of
the Jewish community. It was more inclusive racially. In
the first century Judaism had attracted many who were
not Jews by race, but it had insisted that to partake of the
full blessings of the promises made to Israel these must
become Jews. At first some Christians were of the same
mind. Long before the close of the fifth century, however,
the majority of Christians had rejected this view. They
insisted that, although the Christian community was built
on the foundation laid by Jewish seers, in Jesus a new
beginning had been made and that loyalty to Him and the
new life through Him were the chief tie. The characteristic
rites of the Church, baptism and the Lord's Supper or
Eucharist, although having Jewish antecedents, because of
Jesus possessed distinctive forms. Nothing exactly parallel
to the Church has been brought into being by any other
religion. Buddhism speaks of what is sometimes rather
loosely translated as the Church, but this approximates
more nearly to the monastic groups of Christians than to
the entire body of believers, lay, clerical, monastic, and
non-monastic, as is the case in Christianity. In theory and
to a certain extent in practice solidarity exists among the
followers of Mohammed, but it does not show itself in
ecclesiastical bodies such as are the Christian churches.
Ideally the Church has been a community embracing all
Christians, both living and dead.

Not even in the first five centuries did the Church fully
live up to its ideal. Never were all who called themselves
Christians in one visible organization. There were churches,
never one all-inclusive visible Church. Many of the leaders
of these churches were far from embodying the ideals of
Jesus. Repeatedly the churches quarrelled with one
another.

Yet, with all their weaknesses, it was through the
churches that Christianity and with it the influence of
Jesus spread. In spite of their divisions the churches were
fairly closely knit. Each presented a strong front against
the world. By a discipline whose strictness varied from

group to group they sought to enforce their distinctness from the society about them. Their intransigence brought persecution but it also promoted inner solidarity. They displayed a strength which was one of the causes of the expansion of the faith. By A.D. 500, moreover, the majority of the Christians in the Roman Empire were in what called itself the Catholic Church.

During the first three centuries the influence of Jesus was restricted chiefly to the churches. Since they were separate from the world about them and were in antagonism to it, their attempts to mould civilization were confined mainly to their own fellowships. Within these fellowships they constructed societies which in their ethics and many of their customs bore clearly the imprint of Jesus. The distinctiveness in life and worship which set the churches apart from the community about them was one of the assets of Christianity and helped to account for the spread of the faith.

After the adoption of Christianity by the state, in the fourth century, the chief effect was in the area of religion as a cult. Rival cults, with the exception of Judaism, were all but eliminated. Art and architecture were modified and literature continued to be created, but in fields ancillary to the Christian cultus. Ethical practice showed some changes, but the majority of professed Christians had entered the Church through a mass movement and their lives were not greatly altered.

Partly in protest against this lack of conformity of the rank and file of Christians to the teachings of Jesus came what proved to be one of the most persistent channels for the transmission of the influence of Jesus, monasticism. Monasticism was the attempt to follow fully the commands of Jesus. Many became monks from other motives. Some were self-indulgent. Others were bizarre exhibitionists. Even the most sincere monks distorted, although unintentionally, the message of Jesus. Yet in general, monasticism attracted those souls who were unhappy over the easygoing Christianity of the masses and who sought fully to follow Jesus. It was late in the third century before monasticism arose. In the fourth century monks were becoming active in the spread of the Christian faith. It was the leading representative of nascent monasticism in Gaul, Martin of Tours, who became also an important agent in the spread of Christianity in that region. From then until the emergence of Protestantism, with its revolt against monasticism, it was usually monks who bore the chief brunt of introducing the faith to new areas and of instructing the neophytes. Often monks were supported by civil rulers whose motives were of mixed origin and quality. Repeatedly methods were employed which were quite contrary to Jesus. Yet always this central current of monasticism showed, more than the rank and file of Christians, the influence of Jesus and so helped to perpetuate it. To this very day it is largely through monastic congregations or groups of secular clergy conforming in part to monastic standards that Roman Catholic Christianity is spread.

Not all attempts to achieve full loyalty to Jesus as against the compromises of the church of the majority resulted, as did monasticism, in continuing agencies for the spread of the faith. Marcionism, Novatianism, Donatism, and Montanism did not do so. Into the reasons for the failures of these movements we need not go. Monasticism, however, had an enduring life.

Another means of the perpetuation of the influence of Jesus was the New Testament. The collection which we call by that name was only gradually assembled and standardized. In the first five centuries it has a secondary even though in its discreet portions an important part in the expansion of the Christian faith. However, now and later it did much to transmit the memory and teachings of Jesus. It contained the most authentic records of his birth, life, sayings, death, and resurrection, and the documents written by those closest to him in time and sympathy. Regarded, as it was, with reverence, and being read and studied in the churches as authoritative, the New Testament became an instrument whereby Jesus continued to meet generation after generation and era after era.

The New Testament was reinforced by the Old Testament. In spite of the antipathy of the minority headed by Marcion, the majority of Christians adopted the Jewish

Scriptures as their own and interpreted them in the light of what they believed they saw in Jesus. Contending that the entire historical development portrayed in the Old Testament from the creation of the world through the course of the Jewish race found its clue in Jesus, they claimed for their faith an antiquity which proved an asset in meeting the charge that Christianity was an ephemeral child of yesterday and without that dignity of ancient lineage possessed by the philosophies of Greece. In an age which in its distrust of its own reason sought the sanction of the past, the possession of the Old Testament was a means to the spread of Christianity.

Obviously one of the processes by which Christianity spread in this period was the labour of missionaries. We have already suggested that after monasticism appeared monks were among the active missionaries. They had the advantages of the zeal of full commitment to the Christian faith, of freedom from responsibility for wife and children, and of organized fellowship under directing heads. Long before monasticism put in its appearance, however, missionaries, namely those specializing on the propagation of the faith, had been at work. About the vast majority of them we know very little. Even the names of most of them have been lost. Paul is remembered, largely through his writings. We know of a few others. However, no elaborate machinery was developed for their support. There was nothing which resembled the closely integrated monastic orders which were so prominent in the later propagation of the faith, or the countless missionary societies of the nineteenth and twentieth centuries.

Another means of the expansion of Christianity was mass movements. At the outset conversions were by individuals, one by one, or at times by families and small groups. However, religion has traditionally been as much a group as an individual affair. Cities, tribes, and nations have had their cults which have been supposed to contribute to their collective welfare. The genius of Christianity seemed opposed to tribal or national religion. The appeal of Jesus was, in practice, largely to individuals. In its ideal the Church was a supra-national, supra-racial, and supra-class fellowship embracing Greeks and Jews, barbarians, Scythians, bond and free. As time passed, however, entire communities began to enter the churches *en masse* and Christianity tended to become a group affair. It was thus that the conversion of the Roman Empire was completed. The process had begun before Constantine. In about thirty years as a bishop in Pontus, Gregory Thaumaturgos is said to have witnessed the accession to the Church of the vast majority in the territory covered by his see. Beginning with Constantine, because of the favour of the Emperors, the movement was accelerated. The success of Martin of Tours in the fourth century was probably paralleled in many another diocese. One of the most notable of the group conversions was that accomplished in the Kingdom of Armenia, on the eastern borders of the Roman Empire. That event is so shrouded in legend that we cannot obtain a clear knowledge of the details or ascertain the motives. It seems well established, however, that, led by the king and the nobility, within the span of a few years the entire nation adopted Christianity. The shrines and the endowments of the pre-Christian cult seem to have been transferred to the new faith. Under such circumstances the life and teachings of Jesus could have been only a minor factor in the adoption of Christianity, for the multitude could have known little about them. Even many of the priests could have only the most superficial acquaintance with them. It was not until several generations after the formal conversion that through the translation and preparation of literature and through contact with the older Christianity in the Roman Empire an appreciation of the meaning of Jesus grew and deepened.

None of the processes and factors which we have thus far mentioned fully account for the spread of Christianity. We have still to find the reason not only for the triumph of Christianity over its many rivals for the allegiance of the Roman Empire and of the Hellenistic world, but also for the birth and growth of the Church, for monasticism and its continuing vigour, for the existence and quality of the New Testament, and for the power that could bring about the mass conversions. We must ascertain why, of all the many sects of Judaism, Christianity was almost the only one which achieved a permanent separate existence, and why it was the only one which in numerical strength surpassed its parent. Here was a vitality which was not limited to any one race or culture. Although in part identified with Græco-Roman civilization, this was because, being born into the Græco-Roman world, it won that world first and not because by its original genius it was best adapted to it. The fact that, in spite of its early association with that world and of the antagonism felt because of this seeming alliance, Christianity won some adherents from other cultures is evidence of the striking universality and vigour of the impulse which created it. The source of this abounding life could have been no other, as Christians have all along said, than Jesus Himself. It is He who accounts for the Church and the New Testament. It was the loyalty to Him which was the chief source of monasticism and of the contagious conviction which made monks for centuries the chief active agents in the spread of the faith. The mass movements came because of a momentum which had already been given by this original impulse.

Moreover, here was not an impulse which had been once given and was then allowed to fade into oblivion. Through the Lord's Supper and through its teachings and its symbolism the Church strove to bring successive generations into living relationship with its Lord. Through the New Testament it sought to renew in each age the same vivid touch with Jesus that those had had who heard from the lips of the intimates of Jesus the account of their experience with him. As a result, a quality of life has been reproduced age after age, among different races and in different cultures which, while not always the same, always bears a striking family likeness. It is this life, traceable back to Jesus, a life welling up in personal experience but overflowing to work changes in society, which is the main source of the spread of Christianity, not only during the first five centuries but also in all later ages.

Even the most striking failure of Christianity in the first five centuries bears witness to the power and the universality of the appeal of Jesus. The great body of Judaism did not accept Jesus. The faith from which Christianity had sprung was the one religion in the Græco-Roman world which did not succumb to Christianity. Judaism continued, not, indeed, reaching out as aggressively as when Jesus was born, but more closely integrated in the fifth century than it had been in the first. This was partly because of a strength inherent in Judaism and which the Christians inherited. It was to no small degree because of the high ethical monotheism which the two faiths had in common. It was also because of the striking antagonism of Jesus to Judaism. The Ebionites, those who attempted to be both Jews and Christians, had only a feeble existence and dwindled and died. Thousands of Jews became Christians, but the vast majority of them in doing so ceased to be Jews. The reason was not that Christianity had become Hellenized. Hellenistic Judaism disappeared. Presumably Christianity would have vanished had it been simply a Hellenized Judaism. The contrast between Judaism and Christianity was partly between the universality of Christianity, its appeal to all men regardless of race or culture, and the persistent and narrow tribalism of Judaism. This, as Stephen and Paul saw, went back to Jesus himself. The contrast was chiefly because in Jesus, to some extent in His teachings but chiefly in what He Himself was, His death, and His resurrection, and the resulting experience with what Christians termed the Spirit, a novel and revolutionary force had been released. While rooted in Judaism, Christianity was a fresh beginning. This could have been brought about because of nothing else and nothing less than Jesus Himself. It is in Jesus that the source of the vitality and continuing vigour of Christianity must be sought.

CHAPTER II: THE FIRST AND GREATEST RECESSION

A.D. 500—A.D. 950

The great advance which had made Christianity the formal faith of the most populous cultural centre on the globe was followed by a long period of decline which for a time seemed to presage the end of the influence of Jesus. As in the case of many great movements, boundary dates are difficult to determine and at best are only approximate. Earlier ones might be defended for both the beginning and the end of the recession.

The disheartening losses were associated with the decay of the Roman Empire. For that decay Christianity seems to have been in no way responsible. Both at the time and later the blame has been repeatedly laid at the door of Christianity. The fact that the growth of the latter coincided roughly with the rapid increase of the visible signs of the dissolution of the Græco-Roman world has appeared to many to indicate cause and effect. The factors which made for the decline of Rome were many and complex and even now scholars do not fully agree as to what they were. It is clear, however, that at least some of them had begun to operate before Christianity became prominent and possibly before the birth of Jesus. The most that can legitimately be said against Christianity is that it did not arrest and reverse the process. On behalf of Christianity it must be recorded that it was the source of most of such new cultural achievements as were registered in the Roman Empire after the second century. The emergence of the Christian Church, of Christian theology, and of Christian art, shows that what was lacking in the Mediterranean world was not native ability but a sufficiently powerful impulse to stir that ability to creation. It must also be recalled that it was largely through Christianity that such of the cultural heritage of Greece and Rome as survived was preserved and transmitted to future generations.

Although Christianity was not its cause, the decay of Rome seemed to threaten the end of that faith. Christianity was put in jeopardy by its very success. Through its

first great triumph it had come to be so closely associated
with the Græco-Roman world that the disintegration of
the one might well be the precursor of the demise of the
other. Christianity appeared to be identified with the
fading remnants of a passing culture.

The collapse of Rome and the losses to Christianity were
hastened and accentuated by foreign invasions. The decay
of Rome was due primarily to internal factors. It was
accelerated and made spectacular by pressure from without.
From time immemorial the fertile and salubrious Mediterranean Basin had been subject to incursions from its
periphery. During the years of its might the Roman
Empire was able to halt these at the frontiers. Beginning
with the latter part of the fourth century invasion after
invasion penetrated the weakened defences and wrought
havoc in the crumbling world. The long series is usually
said to have begun with the defeat of the imperial armies and
the death of the Emperor Valens at the hands of the Goths
in a battle at Adrianople in A.D. 378. This was followed,
in A.D. 410, by the capture and sack of Rome by Alaric
and his Visigoths, an event which brought dismay throughout the Empire. In Southern Gaul and Spain the Visigoths
soon erected a kingdom. Other peoples, Ostrogoths,
Vandals, Alans, Suevi, Burgundians, Franks, Lombards,
Angles, Saxons, and Huns, entered in the fifth and sixth
centuries. Fortunately for Christianity, some of these were
already adherents of that faith before they established
themselves in the Empire. Others, however, were frankly
pagan. The later invaders were entirely non-Christian.
Wave followed wave. No sooner had partial recovery been
registered than another incursion followed, bringing fresh
disasters. In the sixth century, because of the Angles and
Saxons, Christianity disappeared from much of Eastern
Britain. In the sixth century the Uighurs, from Asia,
established themselves in Central Europe. In that same
century the Avars were the most powerful force in Central
Europe and in the seventh century were strong enough to
attack the chief centres of Græco-Roman culture, Constantinople. In the seventh century came the Bulgars.
They settled in the Balkan Peninsula and also proved a

menace to Constantinople. In the seventh century the Slavs were moving into the Balkan Peninsula and were even effecting settlements in Greece. Late in the eighth century the Vikings, from Scandinavia, began ravaging the coasts of Europe from Germany and the British Isles into the Mediterranean as far east as Constantinople. Before many decades they became the rulers of parts of Ireland, Great Britain, Gaul, and what was later Russia. Each fresh wave of invaders brought fresh destruction, and especially to such centres of culture and repositories of wealth as churches and monasteries.

Even more serious was the Arab invasion of the seventh and eighth centuries. While pagan peoples were pressing in from the north and the north-east, the bearers of a new religion were conquering the south and the south-east. As we are to see in a moment, Christianity proved strong enough to assimilate the pagans. At least it eventually obtained their outward allegiance. The reverses which it suffered at their hands were only temporary. Islam, however, proved a difficult problem. In the seventh and eighth centuries Moslem Arabs conquered about half the coast of the Mediterranean, or, in other words, about half the area in which Christians constituted a majority of the population. In the lands in which it acquired political dominance Islam slowly strangled Christianity. In territories ruled by Moslems Christian churches survived for shorter or longer periods. Indeed, in several areas they are still to be found. In some regions, as in Spain, Portugal, Sicily, and, much later, the Balkans, where political power passed again into the hands of Christians, Islam eventually was either eliminated or weakened. Where Moslems continued in control of the state, Christianity suffered. Even in our own day the decline of some of the Christian enclaves continues. Never, not even to the Russian Revolution or to the scepticism of the nineteenth and twentieth centuries, has Christianity suffered such heavy numerical and territorial losses to any one enemy, and, indeed, to all enemies combined, as it has across the centuries to Islam.

The reasons for these losses are not far to seek. First of all was an extraordinary political situation which gave the

Moslem Arabs their initial opportunity. When the Moslem Arabs, in the first enthusiasm of their new faith, tested out the defences of their neighbours, the two strongest states of the Near East, the Byzantine and Persian Empires, had recently fought each other to the point of exhaustion. The Persians had penetrated the Byzantine realms as far as Palestine and Egypt. The Byzantine forces, staging an amazing recovery, had overwhelmed the Persians. Then, when the Arabs attacked his empire, the Byzantine ruler, Heraclius, seized by one of his strange fits of inertia, did nothing to stop them. Moreover, Syria, the logical outpost against the Arab advance, was unhappy under Byzantine rule and was disaffected, and in Egypt, the next Christian territory to fall, the attempt of the Orthodox Byzantine rulers to stamp out the prevailing Monophysitism had engendered dissension. Once having gained momentum, the Arab Moslem tide rolled on until it had engulfed the north coast of Africa, practically all of the Iberian Peninsula, Sicily, and part of Southern Gaul. In its intrinsic nature Islam had its greatest single asset. With a firm and simple belief in God which could be understood by the humblest and least educated, with a fiery confidence in Mohammed as the supreme prophet of God, with reverence for Jesus but declaring that Christians had misrepresented Him, that He was not the unique Son of God, and that to Mohammed had been given a later revelation, with the type of fatalism and belief in heaven which reinforced ardour in battle, Islam proved the faith of warriors. Many Christians became convinced that its claim to be a later revelation than Jesus was borne out by its astounding military successes. Moreover, Islam, while permitting and even encouraging conversion, punished apostasy from itself with death. One might become a Moslem, but once a Moslem one must never again change his faith. While not usually compelling Christians to renounce their faith, Moslems placed them under such disabilities that many Christians were glad to renounce the Christ for the Prophet.

Christianity has proved more resistant to Islam than has any other faith—unless it be Judaism and Hinduism. The

Zoroastrianism of the Persians all but disappeared or sought refuge in India, but the Christian churches in the former Persian realms lived on under the Arabs and even flourished. Christianity, and through it Jesus, made contributions to Islam. It was Christians who translated much of Greek literature, including the philosophers, into Arabic. Christian artisans seem to have done much to shape the type of architecture which bears the Arab name. Moslem mysticism and asceticism owed much to contact with the Christians.

However, where the Moslems remained in control, as we have said, the Christian churches dwindled. In North Africa the churches which had given such famous names to the faith as Tertullian, Cyprian, and Augustine completely disappeared. Their collapse was probably accelerated by the fact that they had their chief strength in the Greek and Latin elements in the population and had never been deeply rooted in the Berber stock. The former vanished and the latter persisted. Slowly choked by Islam, Christianity gradually faded in about half the area in which at the dawn of the sixth century it was the professed religion of the majority.

It must be noted, moreover, that Christianity, after having been introduced into China in the seventh century, presumably by the Nestorians, had disappeared from that empire by the middle of the tenth century. So far as we can ascertain the reason, it is to be found partly in severe persecutions which were visited on Buddhists as well as Christians and partly in the alien nationality of the Christians and of the Christian leadership. We are not sure that any Chinese became Christians—although it is probable that some did. The monasteries were small and, so far as we know, manned by foreigners. With the decadence of the T'ang Dynasty, in whose prosperous years Christians, with other foreigners, had been attracted to China, the alien groups seem to have dwindled.

Along with the blows dealt by invaders from without went a decline in the inner life of the Church. This decay in morale was neither steady nor uniform. Here and there were revivals. In the Byzantine East an upswing began in the ninth century. In Western Europe, however, the end of the ninth and the opening of the tenth century witnessed a nadir in the vigour of the Church. Irish monasticism, from which had issued currents of life to the British Isles and the Frankish domains, had been brought to a low ebb by the prolonged Norse invasions. The decline of the Carolingian power had left the Papacy, to which Western Europe looked for spiritual leadership, a prey to the worldly nobility of Rome. A series of Popes sat on the throne of Peter the scandal of whose lives was not offset, as was that of some of the most infamous of the Pontiffs of the fifteenth century, by the outward splendour of their court. In Western Europe Christianity seemed dying from within.

The four and a half centuries after the year 500 made it clear that the vitality inherent in Christianity as the legacy of Jesus was not alone sufficient to ensure the spread and survival of the faith. An adverse environment might check it or even kill it.

However, the losses of Christianity in this period, while severe, are by no means the complete picture. There were also gains.

Advances were made in winning fresh peoples and new territories to the Christian faith.

Of the pagan barbarians who invaded the Mediterranean world from the north and north-east all who permanently settled in that region became adherents of Christianity, although the conversion of some was delayed until after A.D. 950. In Western and Central Europe, even in what was, in general, a period of seeming loss, Christianity was carried northward beyond former borders of the Roman Empire and of the faith. In the years when fresh invasions were sweeping new waves of pagans in destructive raids into nominally Christian areas and Arabs were bringing about half of what had been Christendom under the sway of the Crescent, Christianity was recouping some of its losses by conversions in that very Mediterranean Basin and on the borders of what had been the Roman Empire among peoples which until then had been largely or entirely outside its influence. In Gaul the Franks, who made themselves dominant in that area and who later constituted the nucleus of the Carolingian Empire, were baptized and became champions of the faith. The approximate date of the baptism of the first Christian king of the Franks, Clovis, was A.D. 496. Late in the sixth century and in the course of the seventh century the Angles and Saxons, who had wiped out much of the Christianity of Britain, accepted the faith which had once been their prey. From them went missionaries to the Continent. In the seventh, eighth, and ninth centuries such of the Germanic peoples in Western Europe as had not been converted earlier were won. Among these were the Frisians in the Low Countries, the Hessians, and, last of all, the Saxons. Before A.D. 950 some of the Vikings had been baptized. The Avars were converted, largely in the latter part of the eighth and in the ninth century. Beginning at least as early as the seventh century, the conversion of the Slavs had its inception. It was several centuries before the process was completed. In the ninth century a large proportion of Moravians and the Bohemians were baptized. In the ninth century occurred the conversion of many of the Slavs in the Balkan Peninsula, including the Serbs. The ninth and the first part of the tenth century witnessed the conversion of the Bulgars. Here was an amazing achievement, of prime importance for the future of Christianity.

It was not only among the invaders of the Mediterranean Basin that advances were registered in these dark centuries. Christianity also spread southward and eastward. Beginning in the sixth century, it gained footholds up the Nile, in Nubia. It augmented the hold which it had earlier acquired in Ethiopia. Jacobites and Nestorians and even Greek Orthodox were to be found in Central Asia. The Nestorians, as the chief of the churches in the Sassanian and then the Abbasid realms, led in the propagation of the faith in the East. In the sixth century Christian communities existed on the Oxus. There were Christians among the Hephthalite Huns and the Turks. Christianity became strong in the cities of the valley of the Jaxartes. It moved eastward across the mountains into the Tarim River Valley and in the first half of the seventh century was planted in China. Manichæism, which honoured Jesus and in which Christian influences were present, was widespread in Central Asia and was represented in China by small communities. Christianity continued in India, although we know too little of its early history there to be clear whether in these four and a half centuries its gains offset its losses. As early as the sixth century there were Christians in Socotra, not far from the entrance of the Gulf of Aden, and by the ninth century that island is said to have been Christian.

In spite of the prodigious numerical losses, the largest proportionately which Christianity was to know, and in spite of the wars, the disorder, and the collapse of the empire with which Christianity had been most closely associated, by A.D. 950 Christian communities were scattered over a broader area than they had been in A.D. 500. With them, the influence of Jesus had become more widely disseminated.

The causes of the expansion of Christianity in these difficult centuries were varied. Some of them were more obviously opposed to the spirit and teachings of Jesus than had been any of the agencies of spread in the preceding five centuries. Others, if not so manifestly contrary to what Jesus had stood for, were not intrinsically friendly to it.

Much of the conversion occurred as part of the assimilation of barbarians to the culture of the regions which they had invaded. While mastering a region, the conquerors wished to enjoy it and to take advantage of the civilization which was there. By the sixth century the Roman provincials were generally Christian. Naturally the barbarian invaders from the north and north-east tended to drop their paganism and to assume the Christian name. This factor seems to have made powerfully for the conversion of the Slavs who settled in Greece and Macedonia. It appears to have been potent in the conversion of the Franks. Undoubtedly it was largely responsible for the exchange by the Goths of their Arian Christianity for the Catholic Christianity which prevailed about them.

The expansion of Christianity often coincided with a time of prosperity of a realm which was professedly

Christian. Thus the revival of the Roman Empire under Justinian was accompanied by the spread of Christianity on the borders of his territories, notably into Ethiopia, in North Africa, in Arabia, and in the Caucasus. The Carolingian monarchy, in the eighth and ninth centuries the strongest political force in Western Europe, and a champion of Catholic Christianity, was partly responsible for the halting of the Moslem Arab advance from the south and the conversion of some of the peoples on its northern and eastern marches. A renewal of the power of the Byzantine Empire in the eighth century was to some degree accountable for the acceleration of conversions in the Balkan Peninsula.

The zeal and leadership of civil rulers was often very important. As the espousal of Christianity by Constantine and his successors had speeded up the conversion of the Roman Empire, so the adoption of Christianity was hastened or made possible by the favour of many another monarch. Although Clovis did not employ force to induce his Frankish followers to conform to his example, his baptism gave a powerful stimulus to that of his nation. Again and again in Great Britain the conversion of one of the Anglo-Saxon kingdoms followed upon that of its king. The Carolingians accorded active backing to missionaries among the Frisians and in the Rhine Valley. Their motive may have been partly religious, but obviously the acceptance of Christianity from agents who were under their aegis would make for the extension of their authority. The support of Christianity, therefore, became a method of Carolingian imperialism. More than one Slavic prince engineered the conversion of his subjects. The conversion of the Bulgars was accomplished largely because of the initiative of their king, Boris, and the leadership of his great son, Simeon.

Among the Slavs the desire of the Germans to spread their authority was a complicating factor. It may have been fear of German aggression which led the Moravian Slavic prince, Rastislav, to send to Constantinople for missionaries. Certainly Cyril and Methodius, who came in response to this appeal, met persistent and bitter opposition from the Germans, including particularly the German clergy. Again and again German priests and monks insisted that missions among the Slavs on their eastern borders must be conducted by them, and opposed the use of translations of the sacred books and the liturgy into Slavonia, presumably because it would encourage Slavic political and ecclesiastical independence of their rule.

Occasionally armed force was employed to ensure the acceptance of baptism. Famous was the use of it by Charlemagne among the Saxons. Both Charlemagne and the Saxons evidently regarded the reception of baptism as tantamount to acquiescing to his authority and becoming incorporated into his realms. After he had reduced them to submission, the Byzantine Emperor Basil I compelled the Serbian pirates of the Narenta Valley to be baptized.

We must remember, moreover, that more than once force saved Christianity from grave territorial losses. It was the Battle of Tours which stemmed the Moslem Arab advance. The armies of the Byzantine Empire were long a bulwark against the Moslem tide which, but for them, might have engulfed much of Western Europe. However incompatible the spirit of Jesus and armed force may be, and however unpleasant it may be to acknowledge the fact, as a matter of plain history, the latter has often made it possible for the former to survive.

Commerce was a factor. The spread of Jacobite and Nestorian Christianity in Central Asia largely followed the trade routes. Christianity was strong among the merchant population of the cities of Mesopotamia. Christian merchants, journeying eastward, carried their faith with them. It is more than a coincidence that Christian communities existed in such caravan centres as Merv and Samarkand. Christian merchants were among the pioneer representatives of Christianity in Scandinavia. The planting of Christianity in Southern Arabia seems to have come as a concomitant of commerce. The strength of what was known as Syrian Christianity in the regions of India in which were the marts of sea-borne commerce is probably evidence of the close connection of the origin of that faith with the trade with Mesopotamia.

Sometimes what many Christians would call superstition led men to the baptismal font. Miracles were confidently believed and reports of them aided the spread of the faith. For instance, the visit of the English Bishop Wilfrid to the Frisians in A.D. 678 and his preaching coincided with an unusually large catch of fish and peculiarly fruitful harvests. These were attributed to his presence and encouraged the reception of baptism.

It was not alone factors indifferent or even antagonistic to the temper of Jesus and His message which accounted for the spread of Christianity in these parlous centuries. Within Christianity and deriving ultimately from Jesus was a vitality without which the faith would not have persisted or have won fresh converts.

The active missionaries who preached, baptized, and taught the neophytes were usually monks. Monks, it will be remembered, were Christians who, at least in theory, had given themselves fully to the commands of Jesus. Obeying what they believed to be his behest, they had left all to follow him. To be sure, monasteries often lost their pristine devotion and became centres of easy living and even of vice. Many were attracted to them by the hope of security and quiet in a disorderly age. However, this decay in devotion was usually after the initial hardships of breaking ground for the faith and founding the monastery had passed. In the pioneer stages, it was usually the more sincere and singlehearted who bore the brunt of missionary effort. They did not perfectly conform to the standards of Jesus. Some of them were attracted by the opportunity for adventure or were moved by dissatisfaction with their lot in the parent monastery. Yet in general it was those who were most ardently loyal to Jesus as they understood Him who were the outstanding pioneers and who were most honoured by succeeding generations. The very fact that their memory was revered tended to perpetuate the life which they were believed to have embodied. Thus Martin of Tours, who, to judge by the number of churches named after him, was an inspiration and model of many an ecclesiastic and layman, was remembered by a friend and admirer as never angry or annoyed or mournful and as having nothing in his mouth but Christ and nothing in his heart but piety, peace, and pity. It was just at the dawn of this period, so generally a time of recession for Christianity, that one of the great monastic movements came into being. It was in the sixth century that Benedict developed the rule which long gave Western monasticism its characteristic form. The Benedictine rule, with its alternation of work and worship, was more activistic than was most of Eastern monasticism. The Benedictine houses which were dotted over much of Western Europe became centres of learning and of the arts of peace and often were aggressively missionary. They strengthened the tradition, probably in part an expression of the practical Roman spirit and partly derived from Jesus himself, which made Christianity in the West a more effective force for moulding civilization than was Christianity in the East. Gregory, later named "the Great," who had been caught up in the first flush of the Benedictine movement and had devoted his inherited wealth to the poor and the Church, sent the famous contingent of Roman monk-missionaries to Britain. The Irish monks who had so large a share in the conversion of many of the peoples of Great Britain and of the Continent and did much to revive the Christianity of Western Europe professed to leave home and go upon their wanderings "for the name of the Lord" or "for the love of the name of Christ"—or at least these were among the motives ascribed to them by their biographers. Two of the greatest Irish missionaries, Columban in the Frankish domains and Columba in Scotland, made their original excursion from their homeland with twelve companions, presumably in imitation of Jesus and his apostles. Willibrord, the outstanding English missionary to the Frisians, drew his inspiration from the Irish, and his original band to the Low Countries numbered twelve. The monk Boniface, the chief missionary in the Rhine Valley, turned his back upon assured ecclesiastical position in England for the perils of a pioneer and left a profound impression of courage, selflessness, and beauty and strength of life. It was Anskar, a monk who had already been one of a ground-breaking group in the land of the recently converted Saxons, who became the head of the perilous Frankish enterprise for winning the piratical Scandinavians.

The chief agency for the perpetuation and propagation of Christianity in these dark centuries was that unique creation of the Christian spirit, the Church.

In some respects the Church profited by the collapse of the Roman Empire. In the East, in the Byzantine realms, where the power and tradition of the Roman state survived in a continuous succession from the Cæsars, the Church, true to the traditional position of the official religion of the Empire, was kept subordinate and ancillary to the state. To be sure, it maintained much of the structure which it had developed before it was adopted by the state, and, in general, it was less subservient than the state cults which had preceded it. Not all of its independence was quenched. Yet it tended to be an arm and tool of the state. In contrast, in Western Europe, where the political structure of the Empire suffered more than in the East and in several regions disappeared, the Church survived and took to itself some of the powers and functions of the Empire. It had an ecclesiastical structure more comprehensive geographically than that of any single state and acknowledged allegiance to a single directing head, the Bishop of Rome. For generations the Byzantine Emperors preserved their hold on diminished portions of the Roman domains in the West. Charlemagne attempted to revive the Empire in the West and he and some of his successors bore the imperial title. In the tenth century Otto I was crowned Emperor, a step which is usually regarded as the inauguration of the Holy Roman Empire. Yet the Byzantine dominion in the West dwindled and neither Charlemagne nor the Holy Roman Emperors obtained the extensive control over the Church which their Byzantine counterparts exercised in the East. In spite of some palpably unworthy and weak men who obtained the See of Peter, the power of the Papacy increased, enhanced by the decay of the imperial authority and by its double heirship to the great name of Rome and to the prestige of Peter and Paul and built up by an occasional Pontiff of outstanding ability. Even apart from the Papacy, although in practice that separation was not made, the Church in the West remained the most stable institution in an age of disorder when civil authorities came and went and violence was rampant. Thus in the first centuries of the invasions of Gaul the bishops, recruited largely from the Gallo-Roman aristocracy, stood for order and were the protectors of the weak. It was chiefly through the Church and its monasteries that such education and learning as survived was handed down to later generations, that the poor were succoured, that the marriage tie was given sanctity, that the sick were cared for, that travellers were sheltered, and that morality was inculcated. To be sure, ecclesiastical offices were often the prey of men who were attracted by their power and wealth. Both higher and lower clergy often grossly caricatured or in effect spurned the Christian ideal. In times of grave civil disorder the morale and quality of the Church sometimes sank to a low ebb. Yet the Church went on, the most nearly stable and inclusive institution in an age when war was chronic and only a few of the strongest princes could establish, and then only temporarily and over a limited area, some semblance of order.

This perseverance of the Church was due primarily to its inward spiritual strength. It was not from the momentum acquired in the days when the Roman Empire was intact. Had the latter been the explanation, the Church would have collapsed with the Empire or at best would have survived it but a few generations. The Church went on, the source of continuing life and even in the Dark Ages the well-spring of new movements. In spite of temporary recessions it was a growing power. That this was the case must be ascribed to the strength of the original impulse out of which the Church arose. It was due, in the last analysis, to Jesus Himself.

It is, however, significant that this impulse from Jesus issuing in a vigorous church was most potent in the conditions peculiar to Western Europe. It persisted in the Byzantine Empire, but not so markedly, apparently because it was handicapped by a strong even though ostensibly friendly state. It was unable to make much headway in the Persian realms where the espousal of Zoroastrianism by the state restrained it. In general it lost ground in areas where Islam held the reins of political power. It was in Western Europe, where it faced a much weaker paganism, was associated with the prestige of Roman civilization, and, while often favoured by civil rulers, did not have to confront a continuously powerful state which controlled all phases of life, that the influence of Jesus was most marked. Inner vitality was essential to survival, but it was not enough. The environment also had to have favouring features. In this age of the major recession of the faith it was the combination of inner vitality and environment which made possible the persistence and the growing power of Christianity in Western Europe. It was in the one area in which states professedly friendly to Christianity were not strong enough to bring the Church completely to heel that the influence of Jesus was most effective. It was from this area that it chiefly went on to future ages and that it had its major geographic expansion.

CHAPTER III: THE SECOND GREAT AGE OF ADVANCE

A.D. 950–A.D. 1350

Even before A.D. 950, movements were beginning to appear which were to mark a new major age of advance in the influence of Jesus. In the next four centuries that influence was to mould an important culture more profoundly than ever it had moulded a culture before and was to expand more widely geographically than at any previous time.

The surge of life was most pronounced in Western Europe, that region in which, as we suggested at the close of the last chapter, because of a combination of factors, the influence of Jesus was less restrained and more nearly had free course than elsewhere.

The new life was evidenced in part by fresh religious awakenings which sought to bring the Church more nearly into conformity with the teachings of Jesus. In A.D. 910 the monastery of Cluny was founded and soon became the centre of a widespread effort for the reform of monasticism. The revival associated with the name of Cluny extended its efforts beyond the monasteries. It endeavoured to free the Church from "simony," the sale and purchase of ecclesiastical office by money or other unworthy reward. It strove for a celibate clergy. By these two measures it would improve the leadership of the Church.

Before the end of the tenth century the reforming impulse had placed better Popes on Peter's chair. In the eleventh century the reforming party put a series of great Pontiffs on the throne and devised a method of election which it was hoped would free the Papacy from that control by the Roman nobles which had contributed to bringing it to its low ebb of the tenth century. One of these Popes, Hildebrand (Gregory VII), fought the strongest monarchs of Western Europe, the Holy Roman Emperors, to free the Church from the domination of the secular arm by which it was chronically threatened. It was at the close of the twelfth and at the opening of the thirteenth century, under Innocent III (1198–1216), that the Papacy reached the acme of its power. Innocent III sought to make the

Church and with it the voice of Jesus supreme in Western Europe. Some of the strongest of the monarchs were constrained to make concessions to his claims, and he brought John of England into humiliating surrender and induced him to acknowledge that realm a fief of the Papacy.

Reform movements multiplied, striving for a purer embodiment of the Christian spirit. Some of these, like Cluny, expressed themselves in a stricter monastic life. Among them were the Cistercians, the Camaldulians, the Vallombrosians, the Carthusians, and the Premonstratensians. Others, notably the Dominicans and the Franciscans, displayed some of the features of the older monasticism, but were more active in carrying the Christian message to the masses and in seeking both to raise the level of the living of professed Christians and to carry the Christian message to non-Christians. Still other movements were so radical and were so independent of the church of the majority that they were adjudged to be heretical and were persecuted. Among these were the Poor Men of Lyons, who took their rise from Peter Waldo, and the Cathari.

The Western Europe of these four centuries bore on more phases of its culture the impress of Jesus than had Græco-Roman civilization at the earlier high-water mark of Christian influence. In the Græco-Roman world the great achievement of the Christian spirit had been the erasure of the pagan cults and the creation of the Church and of Christian literature and theology. Large phases of life outside the Church and beyond what is usually deemed the strictly religious field had been but little affected. Now the imprint of Christianity was visible in every major aspect of the new culture which arose in Western Europe. This does not mean that the culture of the European Middle Ages was Christian, if by Christian is meant full conformity to the teachings and spirit of Jesus. It was not. Much in it was patently and flagrantly a denial of all that Jesus stood for. There was a large amount of practical scepticism. War was chronic. The strong oppressed the weak. Superstition was rife. Yet there was a more thoroughgoing effort to transform and inspire all of life by the Christian faith than there had been in the Græco-Roman world. The

new culture largely grew up under the ægis of the Church.
It was the Church which sought by its teaching and its
penances to inculcate and enforce ethics. Most of the
schools were under the Church, and in much of Western
Europe the clergy were long the only lettered class. The
universities which began to emerge in the thirteenth century were mainly, especially those in Northern Europe, the
creation of churchmen. The chief subject of study, the
one which engrossed the finest minds, was theology. Under
the stimulus of the Christian faith imposing systems of
thought arose, notably the "Summa Theologiæ" of Thomas
Aquinas. The greatest poet of the Middle Ages, Dante
Alighieri, left as the outstanding creation of his genius his
"Divina Commedia," built around conceptions of Christian
origin and unmistakably a product of Christianity. Monasteries were long the chief depositories and reproducers of
books. Monarchs were crowned by religious ceremonies
inspired by Christianity and took oaths in which the
Christian element was strong. Laws showed the effect of
the Christian heritage. In the Truce of God and the Peace
of God the Christian conscience sought, and with some
effect, to reduce and regulate the warfare which was so
constant. The attempts to fix and to enforce a just price
and to prevent the charging of interest on loans sprang
chiefly from Christian idealism. The care of the sick, the
poor, the aged, and the orphans was largely in the hands
of religious organizations and was inspired by Christian
charity. The sense of a common European community
had its major source in the conviction that there were
Christian peoples and that all Christians should be included
in one fellowship, "Christendom." On the basis of this
conception came the later international law.

During these centuries this Western Christendom was
expanding its territories and propagating its faith. The
geographical extension which, in spite of adverse conditions, had been going on in the preceding centuries, continued without a break. The Scandinavians accepted the
faith. Their conversion, especially of those who had settled
outside Scandinavia in lands which were professedly
Christian, had begun before A.D. 950. In the latter part

of the tenth and in the eleventh and twelfth centuries Denmark, Norway, and Sweden became officially Christian. Iceland, peopled by Scandinavians, also accepted the faith. The Scandinavian settlements in Greenland were Christian and had a bishop. The imperfectly known Scandinavian adventurers to North America probably carried the faith to that continent and may even have baptized some of the Indians and Eskimos. The conversion of the Slavs who bordered the Germans on the east was completed—notably of the Bohemians, the Poles, and the Wends. The peoples on the eastern and southern fringes of the Baltic were brought to the faith, although it was well into the fourteenth century and after the close of this period that the formal conversion of the last of them, the Lithuanians, was accomplished. The Magyars, who in the ninth century had been a major pagan menace, late in the tenth and early in the eleventh century were welded into an officially Christian state. Missionaries from Western Europe, especially from Italy, traversed much of Asia from the Near East to China, and here and there gathered small bodies of Christians.

Christianity also spread from the Byzantine Empire. The conversion of Russia was begun through the baptism of the Scandinavian-descended rulers of Kiev and continued throughout and beyond this period. Christianity in Serbia was deepened and the Serbian Orthodox Church was fully organized.

In Central Asia and the Far East, Nestorian Christianity had a wide extension. There were Christians among the Turkish Keraits, the Tartar Onguts, and the Uighurs of Chinese Turkestan. Largely through intermarriage with the Keraits, some of the ruling Mongols were professedly Christian. Nestorian Christians were numerous on the edges of China and, in the thirteenth and fourteenth centuries, within China itself. For a time it seemed not beyond the range of possibility that the Mongols, the conquerors of much of Asia and Eastern Europe, might become officially Christians. That at least was the dream of some Christians of the thirteenth century.

By A.D. 1350, then, Christianity and the influence of

Jesus of which it was the vehicle had reached a new high-water mark. In Western Europe, in spite of the unpromising outlook six or seven centuries before, it had developed its strongest centre. There religious movement after religious movement evidenced its vitality. There it entered more generally into the shaping of culture than it had in any other culture up to that time. Geographically Christianity was scattered over more territory than it or any other faith had ever been. Christians were to be found from Greenland and possibly North America on the west to China on the east and from Greenland and Iceland in the north to Nubia, Ethiopia, Socotra, and Southern India in the south.

It must be noted that, in point of influence, Christianity was as yet by no means the leading religion of mankind. To be sure, in geographic extent it surpassed all others. However, Western Europe, in which it was most potent, was not so prominent as it was to become in later centuries. China, predominantly Confucian, Buddhist, and Taoist, India, prevailingly Buddhist and Hindu, and the Moslem world loomed much larger in the total picture of contemporary civilization. Western Europe was relatively insignificant. The Christian Byzantine Empire, although boasting Constantinople, one of the great urban centres of commerce and culture, was politically a third-rate power and was waning. Over most of the vast area across which it had been carried, Christianity was represented by small minorities sprinkled among non-Christian majorities. In one respect Christianity was not proportionately as outstanding as in A.D. 400. In the latter year it had been the faith of the Roman Empire, which was then still the strongest and most populous state on the globe. In A.D. 1350, although diffused much more widely and having impressed itself more deeply upon Europe than it had upon the fifth-century Græco-Roman world, it was not professed by a cultural centre which was so outstanding as the Roman Empire had been. In spite of this important qualification, the thirteenth and fourteenth centuries witnessed the greatest effect of Jesus upon the human race that had thus far been recorded.

The means by which Christianity achieved this position were, as usual, varied. In these means were also to be found at least some of the causes for its gains. They were largely a continuation of those which had been responsible for the advances which had been registered in the preceding period.

The prestige of the culture associated with Christianity probably had much to do with the acceptance of the faith by the peoples of Northern Europe. The civilization with which these peoples had their most intimate contacts, that on their south, was ostensibly Christian. When they adopted this higher civilization, as they naturally wished to do, as a part of the process of acculturization they accepted Christianity. This appears to have been an especially potent factor in the conversion of the Scandinavians and the Magyars.

The initiative of monarchs and princes was fully as important as in the preceding period. It was usually these, the natural leaders, through whom acceptance of the faith was accomplished. Some of the rulers seem to have been actuated by a genuine, even if not always understanding, zeal for the Christian faith. Some of them appear also to have been moved by political considerations. It seems fairly clear, for example, that Olaf Tryggvason and Olaf Heraldsson, the kings who were largely responsible for the conversion of Norway, used their advocacy of the faith to built up the royal power against the nobles. The latter had as part of their perquisites the control of the local pagan shrines. By abolishing paganism the Olafs would reduce the functions of the chieftains and enhance their own authority. So, too, Kings Geisa and Stephen of Hungary carried on simultaneously the conversion of the Magyars and the welding of them into a unified monarchy. Presumably the resistance of members of the old nobility was as much due to dislike for the curtailment of their position by the new political order as it was to hatred for the new faith. In Poland under Boleslaw Chrobry the extension of royal power and of territory went hand in hand with the spread of the faith, and presumably the pagan reaction which followed Boleslaw's death was directed against Christianity as a bulwark of the innovating political order.

Imperialism was one of the chief agencies for the propagation of Christianity among the Slavs on the German borders. Even more than in the preceding period the Germans backed with force their efforts at conversion. From the time of Henry the Fowler and Otto I, strong German monarchs used baptism and the furtherance of an ecclesiastical establishment to extend their rule over the Wends on their northern marches. The Wends fiercely and stubbornly resisted, and the final triumph of Christianity was accomplished more through colonization by Germans and the extermination or assimilation of the Wends than by the voluntary acceptance of baptism. The exploits of the Knights of the Sword and the Teutonic Knights in subjugating to German power and German Christianity and culture the peoples on the Baltic south of the Gulf of Finland are one of the commonplaces of medieval history.

The association of Christianity with imperialism was not confined to the Germans. The spread of Christianity in Finland was a phase of the Swedish conquest. For a time German imperialism and missions clashed on the Baltic with the more weakly supported Danish commercial, political, and ecclesiastical ambitions. The first successful missionary efforts among the Pomeranians were at the initiative of a Polish ruler who wished in this fashion to extend his domains.

A spectacular form of the spread of Christianity through imperialism and armed force was the crusades. It need scarcely be said that Christianity was not the only or even the chief cause of these expeditions. The crusades were really one phase of the expansion of Northern and Western European peoples, a continuation of the invasions of the Mediterranean world which had been in progress since the fourth century and precursors of the later movements which were to carry European peoples over the globe. Many factors, economic and political as well as religious, produced them. Yet the avowed purpose of the crusades was connected with Christianity. In spite of the attention which they attracted and the effort which went into them, it is doubtful whether they helped as much as they hindered the geographical extension of the faith. They facilitated the planting of small Christian communities in the Near East, some of them mercantile and some, more ephemeral, military, and a few conversions can be traced to the channels opened by them. However, they dealt a serious blow to the already weakened Byzantine Empire, that outpost of Christendom against Islam, and prepared the way for its later conquest by the Crescent. The crusades which were not waged against the Moslem, such as those against the pagan Wends and the heretic Cathari, accomplished something in the extirpation of those against whom they were directed, but it is difficult to believe that they did much to advance the spirit of Jesus—even though they may have promoted the acceptance of Catholic Christianity.

More than in any other period armed force was deliberately employed for the extension of the Christian faith. The use of the crusade, a war consecrated by the Church, became a characteristic device of the Middle Ages. The crusades began in the eleventh century, and while later attempts were made to invoke them, before the middle of the fourteenth century they had passed their heyday. The resort to armed force to effect conversions was not confined to formal crusades. Charlemagne had begun it in the eighth century. Again and again we read of it. There were those who knew that the spirit of Jesus could never be communicated in this fashion and who said so. They, however, were a minority. In earlier centuries armies and navies had sometimes opened the way for Christianity. In later centuries they were repeatedly to do so. Usually, however, wars in whose wake Christianity spread had other objectives which were primary. The propagation of Christianity was at most only a secondary purpose and, with some exceptions, followed as a result unplanned by the generals and admirals. It was chiefly in the four centuries between A.D. 950 and A.D. 1350 that war was resorted to on the ground that it was for the propagation of the faith.

At their outset and for the first three or four generations, the Mongol conquests made for the expansion of Christianity. To be sure, the enormous destruction of life with which they were accompanied dealt blows to Christian communities in some regions, notably in Central Asia. In Russia the Church suffered for a time. However, at the beginning of their rule the Mongols were religiously tolerant and were not given to religious persecution. Some of the tribes which they conquered or forced into alliance with themselves contained Nestorian Christians. Through marriage Christianity entered the ruling house and several of the Mongol princes were baptized as children and were reared as nominal Christians. By bringing under their sway the areas across which went the caravan routes from the Near to the Far East, the Mongols facilitated commerce. With commerce went missionaries. Under Mongol rule Nestorian Christianity re-entered China, and Roman Catholic Christianity for the first time was carried to that land. In Russia the Mongols favoured the Church. Moreover, Christian Russians, seeking escape from Mongol rule, pushed the frontiers of their settlement northward, taking their faith with them. For a time, too, the Mongols in the Near East were inclined to court Western Europeans, whom they found ensconced in the crusaders' fortresses, as allies against the Moslem powers and so were not unfriendly to Christianity. However, after the fall of Acre (A.D. 1291), the last of the strongholds of the crusaders in Syria and Palestine, they seem to have made up their minds that Western Christians were a broken reed and their approaches to them ceased.

Commerce facilitated the spread of Christianity. It was German trade which opened the way for the early missionaries to some of the Baltic peoples. The commerce of the Italian cities aided in the establishment of Christian communities, even though these were primarily of alien merchants, in the Moslem Near East, and assisted in the passage of missionaries to that region. Italian commerce to the Far East made possible the introduction of Roman Catholic Christianity and missionaries to China. The Polos, Italian merchants, stimulated Khubilai Khan to ask

the Pope for teachers of science and religion. Although
no missionaries reached China in direct response to this
request, it was in company with an Italian merchant that
John of Montecorvino, the first Roman Catholic missionary
whom we know to have entered that realm, reached
Cathay. Christian merchants aided some of those who
followed him.

As in the preceding period, however, the spread of
Christianity was not due solely to these adventitious factors,
some of them contradictory to the teachings and temper
of Jesus. The active agents who preached and taught the
faith were almost always monks or friars. It was by secular
rulers that Christianity was propagated in Scandinavia,
sometimes forcibly and for political quite as much as for
religious purposes, but it was largely through English
monks that most of the labour of baptizing and instructing
the neophytes and introducing a continuing church life
was accomplished. Much of Britain had been conquered
by the Vikings, and the latter, as they became Christian,
were willing to see English priests, from whom they need
fear no connection with foreign imperialistic aggression as
they did from the German clergy, come to their realms.
It was largely by monks that the active missionary efforts
among the peoples of the eastern shores of the Baltic were
made. Stephen of Hungary used monks to assist him in
the conversion and instruction of his people. He corre-
sponded with the Abbot of Cluny and so was in close touch
with the currents of the most earnest Christian living of
his day. After their inception Franciscans and Dominicans
were the chief Roman Catholic missionaries to Asia. It
was Franciscans who carried Roman Catholic Christianity
to China. It was monks who were the pioneers of Russian
Christianity in its northern advance. Often after Christianity had been planted in a new area and had been
formally accepted by a people, monks, by founding fresh
monasteries, established centres for the perpetuation and
the deepening of the faith that had been adopted. Monks,
we need again to remind ourselves, were those who in
theory had given themselves most fully to the Christian
ideal, and the friars were at once the products and the

agents of one of the great revivals of devotion to the Christian faith.

As in the preceding periods, the chief channel for the continuation of the influence of Jesus was the Church. The monastic movement, at first held in suspicion by the organized Church, had long since been accepted by it and included within its fold. It was through the parish clergy, most of them not monks, that the Church, its message and its ministrations, were brought to the rank and file of Christians. Although often in conflict with the monasteries, the episcopate, developed in the first few centuries of the Christian movement, remained the chief form of ecclesiastical administration.

As we pointed out at the close of the last chapter, it was in the Church in Western Europe that most of the new life of the period was manifested. It was through that portion of the Church, moreover, more than through any other, that the geographic extension of the faith was accomplished.

A thoughtful observer of A.D. 500 or A.D. 600 would scarcely have predicted that the main stream of the influence of Jesus would find its channel in Western Europe. To be sure, the presence of Rome and the strong church in that city gave a certain advantage. However, Western Europe was much later in becoming professedly Christian than was the Greek East. The areas longest prevailingly Christian were in the Byzantine realms. Here most of what up to that time had been the greatest Christian literature had been produced. Here the Christianized Roman state remained intact. In the West wave after wave of barbarians, many of them pagans, seemed to be engulfing civilization. If a prophecy had been ventured as to the centre from which Christianity, if it survived at all, would go on, the Byzantine Empire and not Western Europe would probably have been picked.

However, the West possessed a certain geographic advantage. It was situated at the extreme end of Euro-Asia, and the main force of some of the invasions issuing from Central Asia largely spent itself before reaching it. The Byzantine Empire was long a partial bulwark against the Moslem. Isolation was an asset.

Moreover, in the East, in an area in which the Roman Empire had gone on without a break and had become by almost imperceptible stages the Byzantine Empire, the state tended to continue the close direction of all phases of life which had been the growing trend in the centuries in which Christianity was being adopted. Following the precedent of the position of the official cults to which Christianity fell heir, the Church, in spite of some remnants of its former independence, was also dominated by the state. This tradition of state control was carried over into those countries, such as Bulgaria and Russia, into which Greek Orthodox Christianity spread but which were not in the domains of the Eastern Empire. Excluded from much active participation in the life of this world, the Greek Orthodox Church moved in the direction of quietism and the inner life. It placed much emphasis upon the liturgy and the spiritual experience which came through the celebration of the liturgy. This trend may have been in part due to influences which entered Christianity through the Hellenism of the first Christian centuries. However, the relation to the Byzantine state was responsible for much of it.

Most of the other Eastern Churches were even more shackled by the state than were the Greek Orthodox bodies. The majority of them were in Moslem lands. Moslem rulers, while usually tolerating Christianity, regarded the Christian communities as enclaves which must be watched and supervised. They fell into the custom of holding the heads of the churches responsible for the conduct of the members. They felt it necessary to have in these posts men in whom they had confidence. This meant determination of the choice of the ranking ecclesiastics. All too frequently, accordingly, the positions were gained through bribery and political chicanery. At best the chief ecclesiastics had to be circumspect in their relations with the Moslem princes and from time to time to engage in intrigue and to adopt an attitude of servility. With such leadership the morale of the churches inevitably suffered. The Eastern Christians, on the defensive against the dominant Islam, with no hope of gaining and holding converts from

BRITISH LIBRARY

that intransigent faith, were forced to depend on their wits. They acquired, therefore, among their Moslem neighbours the unfortunate reputation of unprincipled cleverness and of trickiness. Adherence to the Christian faith was not a matter of personal choice and conviction, but of heredity. Now and then a convert would be won from Islam, but, if he were caught, his life was the forfeit. Some advances were made by the Eastern Churches, but they were outside the territories in which Islam was the other faith.

The Church in Western Europe, which we may now call by the name of Roman Catholic, enjoyed much greater freedom than the Greek Orthodox or the various Eastern Churches. This, as we have said, was because the earlier collapse of the Roman state in the West left it less trammelled by the secular authorities and because its own vigour enabled it to step into the breach. Probably, too, the Roman genius, entering the Church, helped to make it the spiritualized successor of the Empire. However, this latter would have been impossible had not the Church possessed a vitality sufficient to attract men of ability. The Church became the most comprehensive organization in Western Europe, both geographically and in the functions which it assumed.

The Church of the West was not allowed to live unchallenged by the state. Again and again secular rulers sought to control it within their domains. In each Scandinavian kingdom the monarch insisted on having an archbishop to head the church in his realm independent so far as might be from any external authority, secular or religious. In England and France the struggle between Church and state was prolonged. The contest between the Papacy and the Holy Roman Emperors became one of the classics of medieval history.

Moreover, in countless instances, men who had little or no interest in the spiritual and moral mission of the Church, or in following Jesus, sought and obtained ecclesiastical office for the power or the material emoluments which went with it. Many of these clergy, from lowly parish priests to bishops and abbots, were notorious as contradictions of

Christian ideals. Many others among the higher clergy, and even among the Popes, while not so flagrantly un-Christian, were, because of the very position of the Church, more statesmen than saints, absorbed in secular affairs to the neglect of their religious duties and compromising principle in the interests of practical administration. Through its very success and the prestige and consequent power and wealth which accrued to it, the Church was nearly undone, and the continuation of its true function was threatened. Then, too, we must note that the Roman Catholic Church cast out of its fold and persecuted as heretics some radiant and devoted spirits whom loyalty to Jesus as they understood him made obnoxious to the ruling ecclesiastics.

The influence of Jesus was not always confined to ecclesiastical channels. It spread through such extra-churchly means as folk-tales and great literature by laymen such as Dante.

When these and other qualifying facts are taken into account, the fact remains that in Western Europe the Church was, in general, the instrument through which the impulses which issued from Jesus had freer course than in any other major geographic area. Men never forgot that ideally it stood for him and was designed to represent him. Less handicapped by the state than elsewhere, it was better able to strive to make his teachings effective in all phases of culture.

As from the vantage of the perspective given by the long passage of time we now look back to these pages, it becomes clear that, even in the dark period which succeeded the fifth century, forces were at work which were to make of the Church of Western Europe the chief channel for the continuing Christian stream. The inception of Benedictine monasticism just at the beginning of the sixth century, the rise of Irish monasticism, the strengthening of the Papacy through Gregory the Great, and the spread of the faith among the Germanic peoples, largely through monks and nuns, all were movements of prime significance. The flowering of the European Middle Ages sprang from seed sown in most discouraging times.

The Church and its faith were the chief force binding together in some semblance of conscious unity the chaotic, disintegrated society which succeeded the eclipse of the Roman Empire in the West. That unity can easily be exaggerated, but it was real. Largely because of Christianity and the Church, Western Europe eventually constituted a society. The sense of being a community, although a tragically quarrelsome community, which has come down to our day in Western Europe, was chiefly the creation of the Christian faith and the Christian Church. Through the Church, between A.D. 500 and A.D. 1350, Christianity was built into the life of the West.

Never was that West fully Christian. Always a tension existed between the high calling of Jesus and the actual practice of Western culture. But the tension was there. Men were not allowed to forget Jesus. Always he haunted them and disquieted their consciences. This was because, more nearly than elsewhere, out of what had seemed the irremediable catastrophe of the collapse of the Roman Empire and the order and civilization of which it was the embodiment and the guardian, had come to the Church a freedom and an opportunity such as it did not know elsewhere. It was also because there was within the Church, thanks to the Christian faith, a vitality which inspired and enabled it to rise to the challenge. Without this vitality what became an opportunity would have proved a major disaster.

CHAPTER IV: THE SECOND MAJOR RECESSION

A.D. 1350–A.D. 1500

Following the great advance of the Middle Ages there came a second major recession of the Christian tide. This, like its predecessor, showed itself both externally, in losses of territory, and internally, in a decline in morale.

The area across which Christianity was scattered became greatly reduced. In the extreme West and North, Christianity disappeared from Greenland. If it had ever been present in North America it had vanished from that continent. In the East, Christianity ceased to exist in China. Its passing from the Middle Kingdom was even more complete than in the ninth century, for in that former eclipse it had continued among the non-Chinese peoples on the borders of the empire, whereas now even these latter had abandoned it. The Nestorianism once widely disseminated in Central Asia lost its footholds there and shrank to dwindling remnants in Persia, Mesopotamia, and Southern India. The Jacobites east of Syria suffered even more severely. Christianity was fading out of Nubia. In Egypt it was on the slowly losing defensive. Except for a few captives and foreign merchants it was at last eliminated from North Africa. The Byzantine Empire was crushed, and with its passing went the bulwark which had long shielded Europe from the Moslem advance from the south-east. In the first area to become prevailingly Christian, Asia Minor, the Christian communities became minorities. In Greece and the Balkan Peninsula, where in the preceding two periods the assimilation of pagan invaders had slowly been accomplished, Christianity was on the defensive against a resurgent Islam, and Islam was firmly planted as the faith of the ruling power. The retirement was prolonged. It began about the middle of the fourteenth century and lasted until the closing decades of the fifteenth century.

The Christian geographic retreat was less offset by gains elsewhere than it had been in the previous era of recession. In the shrinkage of its territorial boundaries the losses, too, were more pronounced.

Yet the core of what might be called Christendom suffered less from external aggression than it had between A.D. 500 and A.D. 950. Western Europe, which by A.D. 1350 had become the main stronghold of Christianity, was comparatively unaffected. Proportionately the numerical losses to Islam were not so great as in the seventh and eighth centuries. Christendom was not hammered from all sides, as it had been from the fifth to the tenth century, by non-Christian invaders. The vast losses of territory were mostly in areas in which Christians had never been more than small communities or scattered minorities.

The inner loss of morale was pronounced. Even in the first half of the fourteenth century, the rising French monarchy had humbled the Papacy. Boniface VIII, who in his bull *Unam sanctam* had registered the high-water mark of Papal claims to supremacy over civil rulers, was imprisoned by King Philip the Fair, who was augmenting the French royal authority, and, although soon released, died within a few weeks. The Papacy now fell under the control of France, and from 1309 to 1377 had its head-quarters at Avignon. Avignon was not actually in the French kingdom, but, what counted in the decline of Papal prestige, it was regarded by public opinion as under French influence. There followed, as an aftermath of this "Babylonian Captivity," the great Papal schism which divided the ecclesiastical allegiance of Europe. Two and then three rivals claimed to be the only legal Pontiff. This multiplication of Pontiffs was eventually evolved by a revival of church councils. Much hope was centred on these as a means of reform. Unfortunately they, too, in the weakness of their performance, lost the confidence of much of Europe. When the Papal division was at last healed, the Renaissance was in full swing. The See of Peter fell into the hands of men who were more interested in using it as a power in Italian politics, in aggrandizing the members of their families, or in promoting art and their own personal pleasures than they were in making it effective in furthering the spiritual and moral lift of Europe. The burden of Papal taxation increased. The Papacy incurred the hatred and contempt of millions. With such abuses rife at the top, it is not strange that much of corruption infected the body of the clergy and of monasticism. The Church and the clergy fell into widespread disrepute.

The Renaissance brought with it practical scepticism. Christianity contributed to the Renaissance. Some have declared the latter to have been in its inception largely due to earnestly Christian movements. Certainly Christianity entered into it. The Renaissance was not a revival of unaltered Græco-Roman culture. Yet in it Christianity was not dominant. In the Middle Ages Christianity had taken the non-Christian philosophy which had come down from the Greeks and had subordinated it to a Christian purpose, to help to give form to Christian theology. In the Renaissance the reawakened interest in the art and literature of Greek and Roman antiquity was often directed to Christian themes, but the latter did not loom so prominently as they had in the philosophical awakening of the Middle Ages.

While decay was undermining the morale of the Church in the main centre of Christianity, Western Europe, among most of the Eastern Churches it was even more pronounced. Particularly as the Byzantine Empire succumbed to the Ottoman Turks, the Greek Orthodox Church, next to the Roman Catholic Church the strongest of the Christian bodies, declined.

The reasons for this recession in Christianity were many. The contraction of the physical borders of the Christian communities cannot be ascribed to any one factor. A combination of causes, not all of them interrelated, brought it about. The disappearance of Christianity from Greenland arose from the extinction of the Scandinavian settlements on that island. This, in turn, was caused by the termination of contact with the mother country. The dying out of Christianity in China was largely a consequence of the collapse of Mongol rule. The Mongols were driven out in the second half of the fourteenth century. The advent of a native dynasty was accompanied by the end of the large share which foreigners had in the administration of the land and possibly by the decline of foreign merchant communities. Since Christianity, both Nestorian and Roman

Catholic, was closely associated with these foreigners and was largely alien in membership and leadership, its end followed. In Central Asia, as in China, the Christian communities disappeared so completely that we do not know the story of their death. The peoples among whom Christianity had had adherents became either Buddhist or Moslem. The opposition of Zoroastrian Persia in the early Christian centuries had prevented Christianity from penetrating in force into Central Asia. It was Buddhism and Islam which made the greatest progress. Just how the transition to these two religions was made we do not know. Most of the losses of Christianity were from a resurgent Islam. In Persia, where some of their rulers had once been Christian, the Mongols became Moslems. This was because Islam was already the dominant faith in that region, a favoured position which went back to the conquest of the country by the Arabs and to the consequent displacement of the earlier Zoroastrianism by Islam. In Russia the Mongols adopted Islam, possibly because that was what their kinsmen were doing in Persia. The Turkish peoples of the Near East became Moslem, notably the Ottoman Turks who exterminated the Byzantine Empire and carried the Crescent into the Balkan Peninsula and to the gates of Vienna. A few from the great Turkish family had once been Christian. However, the position which had been won for Islam in Persia and Central Asia by Arab arms accorded to that faith a prestige which Christianity had never enjoyed in those regions. The place gained for Islam on the eastern shores of the Mediterranean by the Arab conquest also gave to that religion a dominance which it never lost. It was natural that Turks cradled in Central Asia or growing up in the Near East from immigrant stock should acquire the prevailing faith of the cultures with which they came in closest contact. The break-up of the Mongol Empire and the wars which ensued helped to terminate the widely extended commerce of Europeans in Asia with which Roman Catholic missionaries had been associated. Over vast areas both commerce and missions ceased. The adoption of Islam by the Mongols also proved inimical to European enterprises, both commercial and religious. It was Islam, advancing up the Nile from the Egypt in which the Arab centuries before had given it pre-eminence, which extinguished Christianity in Nubia and began to hem it in in Ethiopia. Even had there been opportunity, a church so distraught and divided and so honeycombed with corruption as was the Roman Catholic Church of the fifteenth century could scarcely be the source of very active missions.

The decline of morale in the Church was also the outgrowth of several factors. Obviously the churches in the lands which had once been ruled by the Byzantine Empire were on the defensive against the triumphant Turk. Their clergy could hold their posts only through tactful and even servile dealings with their Moslem overlords. In Western Europe the culture which had been associated with the Medieval Church, and which the Church had done so much to create, was breaking up. As at the time of the decay of the Roman Empire the success of Christianity in winning that Empire and becoming largely identified with it proved almost its undoing, so the passing of the culture which the Church had helped to nurture and with which it had unavoidably become closely interwoven proved a menace to the Church and its faith. The rising national states sought freedom from the supernatural Papacy which had bound Western Christendom together either by dominating it or by reducing its power within their borders. Fresh intellectual currents diverted men's interest from the theological and philosophical systems which the medieval mind, under the stimulus of Christianity, had erected.

The question arises as to why medieval culture and society disintegrated. Some of the ideals held for them and towards which many of the noblest spirits strove were high. The conception of a Christendom united under an inclusive Christian state, the Holy Roman Empire, and under an equally inclusive spiritual fellowship, the Catholic Church, if it could have been fully realized, would have saved Europe the horrors of political division and the recurring and disastrous wars which have cursed and still curse that continent. The corporate life which was an ideal of the Middle Ages, with its combination of the recognition of divinely ordained authority and the voice of the people, might have avoided both the extremes of unregulated absolutism on the one hand and unchecked democracy with its mass hysteria and demagogy on the other. It may have been that the ideals were fundamentally impracticable. Certainly both Empire and Church proved unable to bring union and peace. The Empire had all but broken down before the new age with its nation states had dawned. The Roman Catholic Church, while by no means so nearly a phantom as the Holy Roman Empire, had also demonstrated its incapacity to bring into being such a society long before the Protestant revolt tore away much of Europe from its fold. Possibly the decay of the Middle Ages arose from the clash of a high impossible ideal drawn from Christian sources with the actualities of politics and the human scene. Whatever the cause, and it was probably not one but multiform, the Middle Ages passed. With their going Christianity and the continuation of the influence of Jesus were threatened.

Yet the decline of the influence of Jesus in this century and a half can easily be exaggerated. The dark shadows were not all of the picture. Already forces were at work and movements were in progress which after A.D. 1500 were to have fruition in the greatest advance which Christianity had yet experienced.

Geographic gains were being registered. In the Iberian Peninsula Christianity was achieving the most notable recovery of territory from Islam which it has ever recorded. This had begun long before A.D. 1350, but culminated after that year. The Christian princes gradually eliminated the Moslem political power. The last of the Moslem states disappeared in 1492, only about a generation after the Koran had supplanted the Christ in St. Sophia. Along with the political conquest went a gradual conversion to Christianity, some of it by force or thinly disguised force, but much of it as a voluntary acceptance of the faith of the ruling classes. The final elimination of Islam in the peninsula was to wait until the sixteenth and the early part of the seventeenth century, when it was accomplished partly by the expulsion of all who were believed to cherish evidences of loyalty to it. Before the end of the fifteenth century those geographic discoveries were in progress which in the following centuries were to carry Christianity around the world and plant it in areas which heretofore had not known it. Prince Henry had already directed expeditions along the west coast of Africa, America had been reached, and the Portuguese had rounded the Cape of Good Hope. Then, too, on the northern marches of Russian settlement Christianity was continuing to advance and non-Christian tribes were being won. It was late in the fourteenth century that the formal conversion of the Lithuanians, to Roman Catholic Christianity, was effected.

Within Europe new movements were appearing which were to bring the greatest revival that Christianity had known. In the fourteenth century, beginning before A.D. 1350, but gaining in momentum after that year, came a marked development of mysticism, chiefly in Germany, Switzerland, and the Netherlands. Eckhart, Tauler, the Friends of God, the *Theologia Germanica*, John of Ruysbroeck, Gerhard Groot, the Brethren of the Common Life, the monastery of Windesheim and its affiliated houses, and the "Imitation of Christ" were among the more outstanding figures and creations of that movement. In England Wyclif attacked the abuses in the Church, inspired the translation of the Bible into the vernacular, sent out preachers to carry the Gospel message to the masses, and gave rise to the Lollards. In Bohemia John Hus left a following which proved to be one of the contributory streams of the Reformation. In Spain at the close of the fifteenth century reform had begun in the Church, partly through the austere Ximenez de Cisneros, the most prominent churchman of the realm, and partly through the emergence of the Discalced Franciscans. Even more than in the previous major recession, new life was stirring which was to issue in a great fresh advance.

As in the earlier recession, this life was in somewhat unexpected quarters. It was not in Rome or Italy or in Southern France, where Christianity had had its earliest strongholds in the Western world and where the Church had its official centre, that it broke out. It was in Germany, the Low Countries, and among the English, where the faith had been effectively planted in the first dark era, and in Spain which in that age of greatest discouragement had seemed to be lost to a triumphant Islam, that the renewal had its inception. It was, moreover, from recent frontiers of the faith that such geographic expansion as was taking place was being achieved. It was from Russia, just emerging from the Moslem Mongol yoke, that the major advance of Eastern Christianity was being registered. It was from Poland, itself professedly Christian for only a little over three centuries, that Lithuania was won. Portugal and Spain, only recently fully freed from the Moslem yoke, were the leaders in the explorations which opened vast new territories to Christianity. The revival gave the first indications of its presence in unpredictable areas.

CHAPTER V: THE THIRD GREAT AGE OF ADVANCE

A.D. 1500–A.D. 1750

As in the other great ages of advance, so in the era which began in the sixteenth century, the resurgent life within Christianity gave rise to new movements. Now, in the sixteenth and seventeenth centuries, these were probably more numerous and varied than in any previous period of equal length, not even excepting the first two and a half centuries or the twelfth and thirteenth centuries.

As an aftermath of the previous recessions, in A.D. 1500 Christianity was confined mainly to Europe. In Asia and North Africa it was represented by static or dwindling remnants of churches which were encircled and being slowly stifled by a politically dominant Islam or, in South India, by the prevailing Hinduism. In South-eastern Europe, Islam was in the ascendant. Only in Russia was Greek Orthodox Christianity the faith of the state. It was to Western Europe that previous losses had mainly constricted Christianity. Even here, in the second half of the fifteenth century, Christianity faced a future which seemed none too promising. It was threatened by internal decay and by the still aggressive Ottoman Turks, loyal Moslems, who were more powerful than any single European state and against whom, in spite of the frantic efforts of the Popes, discordant Western Europe would not unite. Until the amazing geographic discoveries of the closing decades of the fifteenth century, Western Europe seemed to have only a minor role in the human drama as a whole. In A.D. 1500, Islam, supported by the Turks and by various peoples of Central Asia; Confucianism, the system on which the Chinese Empire, larger and more populous and apparently more highly civilized than all of Western Europe, was based; Hinduism, the faith of the majority of the peoples of India, a sub-continent more varied racially and probably more populous and wealthier than fifteenth-century Western Europe; and Buddhism, with extensive followings in Southern, Central, and Eastern Asia, all loomed larger in human affairs than did Christianity.

Christianity, and with it Jesus, seemed to be a waning force. Even in Europe its days appeared to be numbered.

However, in the course of the fifteenth century movements broke out, chiefly in Western Europe, which were to bring unprecedented reinvigoration to Christianity and were to make it, by A.D. 1750, the most widely influential of the faiths of mankind.

One group of these movements was what is usually called Protestantism. This term is really a misnomer. To be sure, those denominated by that name protested against what they deemed the abuses and corruptions of the Roman Catholic Church. They professed to be reformers, who sought to restore Christianity to its pristine purity. As a matter of fact, however, the movements classified under the comprehensive designation of Protestantism were primarily expressions of a vigour which could not be confined within traditional ecclesiastical moulds. They were departures from the generally accepted Christianity too radical to be tolerated within the existing Church, and, although they strove to reproduce New Testament Christianity, they did not correspond fully, either in organization, ritual, or doctrine, to any of the forms which Christianity heretofore had developed. They were in the stream of historic Christianity and were the products of the life inherent in that faith, but to a large degree they were new creations. Lutheranism, Calvinism, Anabaptism, and Socinianism, although they all paid sincere homage to the New Testament and endeavoured to be true to Jesus, were not literal reproductions of anything which had gone before. They displayed, however, great vitality, and one or another of them or of other varieties of what, following the usual convention, we must label as Protestantism, won the allegiance of the majority of the population of Northwestern Europe. The Protestant branch of the Christian stream continued to give rise to new movements. In the nineteenth century, in its growth and in its effect on mankind, it became even more prominent.

Much of the renewed life remained within the Roman Catholic Church. The doctrines and the chief features of the structure of that body endured fundamentally unaltered, but the morale displayed a marked recovery. New orders sprang into being, bearing resemblances to monasticism but, like the Franciscans and Dominicans, products of the preceding revival, more actively missionary and more aggressive in changing the society about them than had been the earlier orders. Several of the old monastic orders were cleansed and recalled to the standards set by their founders. After a prolonged struggle, the Papal chair was won by the reformers and was filled by men who freed the throne of Peter from the perversions which had scandalized right-thinking men and women. Improvements were made in the education and morals of the parish clergy. Catechisms were prepared to raise the level of the religious life of the laity. The Roman Catholic Church, thus revived and reinforced, held the allegiance of most of Western Europe south of the Rhine and the Danube and east of Germany.

In Russia Christianity, although not so extensively reshaped as in Western Europe, displayed vigour. A patriarchate was established and the conviction grew in the country that Moscow was the "third Rome," the true head of Christendom now that Rome had succumbed to the "Latin heresy" and that Constantinople was subject to the Turks. In the "Time of Trouble," the political confusion which began at the end of the sixteenth century, the Church was the chief unifying institution. Indigenous dissenting sects sprang out of the official church, indications that Russian Christianity had sufficient vitality to produce diversity and originality.

Christianity had a profound effect upon the culture of Europe, and especially of Western Europe. At first sight it seemed that the impression made by Christianity was not so deep as in the Middle Ages. It had been rather obvious that medieval culture had grown up under the ægis of the Church and had been moulded by it. The Renaissance had appeared to mark a beginning of the decline of the influence of Christianity. On more careful observation, however, it becomes fairly clear that between A.D. 1500 and A.D. 1700 Christianity made fully as marked an imprint upon Western Europe as it had in the Middle Ages and, when all phases of culture are considered, much more than upon the Græco-Roman world. The Papacy was not so potent in political and international affairs as in the eleventh, twelfth, and thirteenth centuries, and the Church as a unified ecclesiastical structure was broken by the Protestant secession and did not so visibly as in the Middle Ages bind Western Christendom together. However, through men like Francisco de Vitoria and Hugo Grotius, the Christian conscience gave rise to international law. Machiavelli in his teaching and Richelieu in his practice appeared to be ushering Christianity out from the European political system. Yet Vitoria as the contemporary of the one and Grotius of the other were seeking to apply the Christian conscience to the new situation. Christianity contributed both to the doctrine of the divine right of kings, which was used to buttress the absolute monarchies of the times, and to the theories which made for popular sovereignty and democracy and which limited the power of the monarchs. In the Commonwealth in England and in the struggle which preceded it, Christianity contributed fully as powerfully to the shaping of the structure of an individual state as it ever had in the Middle Ages. As in previous periods, Christianity stimulated care for the sick, the poor, the orphans, and the aged. In the realm of æsthetics it contributed to some of the greatest sculpture, painting, and architecture and was the inspiration of some of the most marvellous music ever composed. In literature it provided several of the greatest writers with themes and vision—Milton among them. It did not stimulate scholars within the Roman Catholic Church to produce theological systems comparable with those of the Middle Ages. It gave rise to no Thomas Aquinas. However, but for it Calvin would never have written his "Institutes" and the other Protestant theologies would not have been. Its effect was not so obvious upon the scientific and philosophical thought of the period as it had been upon the intellectual life of the Middle Ages, but most of the leading minds showed its imprint, even if at times to react against it. Some, like Newton, were devout Christians and may have been impelled by their faith to the achievements for which they are best remembered. Fully as much as in the Middle Ages and very much more than in the Græco-Roman world, the innovations and advances in education were stimulated by Christianity. Christianity unquestionably contributed to the geographic discoveries of the time. Henry the Navigator, for instance, was moved in part by his Christian faith, and Columbus was sustained in his exploits by a courage and purpose derived in no small degree from his Christian heritage.

In the sixteenth, seventeenth, and eighteenth centuries Christianity displayed a prodigious geographic expansion, more extensive than it or any other religion or set of ideas had shown before it. It was carried to the Western Hemisphere. There it was the faith of the European settlers and their descendants and was accepted by the majority of the Indians and by many of the Negroes. It inspired those portions of the Laws of the Indies which were for the protection of the aborigines in the extensive Spanish domains. Most of such education as existed, whether in Roman Catholic or Protestant colonial America, was under the Church or arose out of the Christian impulse. In the Spanish and Portuguese possessions, after the first wave of conquest, it was through benevolent Christian missions that the frontier of white settlement moved forward. In the Thirteen Colonies of the British, groups seeking freedom to practice their Christian faith as they believed it should be lived had a large part in effecting the first settlements and did much to mould the ideals of the future United States. Christianity was planted here and there along the western, southern, and eastern shores of Africa. Thousands of converts were made in India and Ceylon. Courageous missionaries penetrated to distant Lhasa. Efforts to plant the faith, although followed by slight immediate results, were put forth in Burma and Siam. In Indo-China the foundations were laid for numerically strong Christian communities. Christianity was widely disseminated in the East Indies, although, except on a few of the smaller islands, converts were few. The majority of the inhabitants of the Philippines became professedly Christian. Christianity was introduced to Japan and for a time flourished most promisingly. It was reintroduced to China and, so far as we are able to determine, won more converts than in either of the two previous periods in which it had been in that Empire. It spread among the peoples of Eastern Russia and in Siberia.

Of the newly entered lands, it was in the Americas, the Philippines, and Japan that Christianity had its most pronounced effects upon civilization and the collective life of peoples. In the Americas and the Philippines, culture was as extensively shaped by it as in Europe. In an effort to eliminate Christianity, Japan was closed to trade with the Occident, except for attenuated contacts with the Dutch. A policy of exclusion was adopted which did much to shape the temper of the country.

The revival and spread of Christianity took place in spite of the demotion of the Church of Western Europe from its prominence as against the state. This demotion was irrespective of the type of Christianity which prevailed, whether Roman Catholic, Greek Orthodox, or Protestant. The centuries were marked by the development of absolute monarchies. In each of these the Crown extended its control over the Church within its domains. In Roman Catholic Spain and its American colonies and in Greek Orthodox Russia, especially beginning with Peter the Great, this control was peculiarly strong. It was also marked in Roman Catholic Portugal and France, in Protestant Scandinavia and England, and in several of the German states. It was the prevailing trend throughout most of Christendom. Church and state were closely united. The monarchs professed to rule by divine right and used the Church to bolster their power. In the struggle, so acute through the Middle Ages, between secular and ecclesiastical authorities, the former had at last won.

The control of the Church by the state and the decline of the Church as a visible supra-national ecclesiastical structure uniting Western Christendom was not due to Protestantism. It is often assumed that Protestantism, by disrupting the ecclesiastical unity of Western Europe, was chiefly responsible for the disappearance of that spiritual commonwealth which characterized the Western Europe of the Middle Ages. To this disintegration Protestantism undoubtedly contributed. It was not, however, either the main or the decisive factor. Protestantism was much more the result of a disruptive force which was already at work than it was the cause of the division. After the Roman Empire had broken down in the West, the part of Europe which it had formerly ruled, together with the portions, chiefly in the North, which were brought within the orbit of Western culture, was divided into almost innumerable political units. These were partially interrelated through feudalism. Occasionally a state or a dynasty arose which for a time brought some of them under its sway. The Carolingians and the Holy Roman Empire endeavoured to do this for all Western Europe, but with only incomplete success. Monarchs in such lands as England and France struggled to reduce the local magnates, but during the Middle Ages the latter maintained much of their power. Only the Church, co-ordinated under the Papacy, pre-served a comprehensive organization. Thanks to the expansion of the faith, in North-western Europe it even added to its territory. However, as time passed and long before the appearance of Protestantism, monarchs began to overcome the feudal nobility. No king or emperor was strong enough to rule all Europe. Particularism proved too vigorous. Instead, several national states arose ruled by absolute monarchs. This process was already well under way before A.D. 1500, especially in Spain, Portugal, France, and England. Largely because of it, the Papacy was already a waning factor in the political scene. As we saw in the last chapter, the Babylonian Captivity and the Papal schism which brought the Church and its faith into such grave discredit were largely due to the emergence of the French monarchy and to the discontent of rival incipient nationalism and monarchies with French control. The worldly Renaissance Pontiffs, who added further to the disrepute of the Papacy, were one of the causes of the emergence of Protestantism. German, English, and Scandi-navian nationalism contributed to the origin and spread of Protestantism. After the rise of Protestantism, some of the monarchs who were most loyal to the Roman Catholic

form of the faith, notably the fanatically Roman Catholic
Philip II of Spain, were among the most emphatic in their
insistence on the royal control of the Church within their
realms. It was not in a Roman Catholic country, but in
Protestant England and Scotland and in the Protestant
Netherlands that the resistance to the domination of the
Church by the Crown in this age of absolute monarchies
first met with some degree of enduring success. Protestantism made impossible a single ecclesiastical structure for
Western Europe, but even had the outward unity of the
Church in Western Europe been preserved, it is hard to
believe that the Popes, as the spokesmen for that comprehensive body, would have had more voice in international
affairs than they actually possessed or that a more effective
unity of culture would have been preserved. Not much
more community of feeling and culture have existed
between the Roman Catholic portions of Germany and
Roman Catholic France or Spain than between Protestant
England and the Roman Catholic sections of Germany.
The Medieval Church, potent though it was, had not been
strong enough to knit Western Europe into an indivisible
whole. Protestantism was more a symptom and a consequence of that failure than it was a cause. The Roman
Catholic Church had never sufficiently transcended its
Roman and Latin environment or become really catholic
enough to weld all of Western Europe together. When
the great division occurred, it was chiefly the Latinized
South which remained loyal to it.

The failure of the Medieval Church so to permeate
Western Europe as to bind it into a unit under a dominant
ecclesiastical structure may seem an indictment not so
much of the Church as of the Christianity which gave birth
to it. If the Church thus failed in the area in which between
A.D. 500 and A.D. 1350 it admittedly had the freest course,
it might seem that there is that in Christianity and the
influence of Jesus which is basically unable to rise to a
great opportunity.

However, the situation is not so simple as all that. We
must recall that, proceeding chiefly from Western Europe,
Christianity became increasingly potent in the life of

mankind as a whole. Even in Western Europe, Christianity probably had greater effect on culture after A.D. 1500 than in the Middle Ages. We must also remember that the ideals and demands of Jesus are so high that they are never fully followed. They create a tension and produce modifications in social practice and institutions. They revolutionize some individual lives. Others they alter, although not quite so profoundly. Now and again, as in the fields of education, thought, and political theory, they bring about startling innovations. Yet never has a society and probably never has an individual fully embodied them. It may be that this side of the grave they never can and never will. However, that does not mean that Christianity has failed. The measure of the influence of Jesus is not the gulf between His teachings and the practice of individuals and of societies, but the changes which have been produced. Seen against the perspective of nineteen centuries and taking into our purview, as we must, the world as a whole, the influence of Jesus has clearly increased.

Between A.D. 1500 and A.D. 1750, as one result of the prominence of monarchical absolutist states, Christianity and the influence of Jesus persisted and spread more under the direction of the state than at any previous time; more so, even, than in the fourth and fifth centuries after the adoption of Christianity by Rome. Monarchs had an important share in propagating Protestantism in Europe. It was under royal direction that Protestantism became dominant in Scandinavia. It was through royal initiative that the Church of England separated from Rome. In Germany Protestantism owed much to various princes. The reform of the Roman Catholic Church was deeply indebted to various monarchs. Isabella early promoted it in Spain. Charles V wished it and worked for it. In the New World Christianity had its most extensive expansion in this period in the domains of Spain and Portugal. Here the Crown through its many officials directed, controlled, and in large part financed the propagation of the faith. In Africa, India, Ceylon, Indo-China, and China, Roman Catholic Christianity was planted or grew chiefly although not entirely under the patronage of the Portuguese Government. This

supervision was not so thoroughgoing as was the control
by the Spanish and Portuguese Crowns in the Americas,
and the attempts of non-Portuguese to contest it and
of the Papacy to be emancipated from it brought
dissensions which long handicapped the spread of the faith.
In the Philippines the Spanish Crown exercised as absolute
a control over the Church as in Spanish America. In the
East Indies the Christianity was chiefly Protestantism, and
the Church and its missions were mainly financed and
promoted by the East India Company through which the
Dutch managed their enterprises in that area. It was
through the same agency that Dutch Protestantism was
introduced into Ceylon, partly supplanting Portuguese
Roman Catholicism. The Danish Crown helped in bringing Protestantism to India. The Russian state usually
directed and financed the spread of the faith in its domains.
It offered peculiarly attractive inducements to baptism,
such as outright presents, temporary exemption from taxation, and freedom for the serfs and those who tilled the soil.
Whatever else the absolutist states of the period did or did
not do for Christianity, they helped to propagate it.

The zeal of monarchs and civil officials for the spread
of Christianity sometimes arose from a genuine concern for
the religious welfare of subject peoples. Probably more
frequently it sprang from a desire to make the Church and
its faith serve the extension or the strengthening of political
or commercial empire. Frequently the two motives were
mingled. In Spanish America after the first wave of conquest had spent itself, and in the Philippines from the very
start, missions were regularly employed as a means of
extending the frontier. Missionaries, usually supported by
a military guard, went beyond the borders of white occupation, persuaded the natives to settle down, and taught
them the arts of peace and Spanish culture as well as the
Christian faith. When the work of conversion was completed, in theory the missions were "secularized"—that is,
the missionaries, most of whom were "regulars" (members
of orders), were required to give place to the "secular"
clergy, and normal parish administration, such as existed
in districts longer under European rule, was introduced.

Whether under Spanish, Portuguese, Russian, or Dutch imperialism, becoming a Christian was tantamount to submission to the political authority of the foreigner and was part of the process of assimilation to his rule and culture. Frequently, as in the Mexican plateau, parts of Peru, and the Portuguese enclaves in India, to ingratiate themselves with their new rulers the natives hastened to seek baptism and Christian instruction. Sometimes, as in the case of a fisher caste in South India, they asked for Christian teachers as a means of obtaining the protection of the European against some hereditary foe.

In spite of this unprecedentedly large part of absolutist governments in propagating Christianity, probably less force was used to compel the reception of baptism than in the preceding periods. In some instances it was employed, notably against the Jews and Moslems in Spain. The expulsion of unconverted Jews from Spain (1492) and Portugal (1497) and of the Moriscoes, the imperfectly converted Moors, from Spain had not been matched in numbers in previous times. Yet, in general, stark force was not so much invoked as in the Middle Ages.

Christianity expanded in connection with commerce. Sometimes non-Europeans adopted Christianity in the hope of attracting lucrative European trade. That seems to have been one of the reasons for the rapid growth of the faith in some of the districts in Southern Japan. Commerce was often followed by territorial conquest and this by the conversion of the inhabitants of the occupied territory.

Occasionally European imperialism and commerce proved a handicap to the spread of the faith. It was fear of foreign aggression which was the chief cause of the persecution that drove into hiding the Christianity of Japan. That was also back of some of the persecution of Christianity in China and Ceylon. In India the English East India Company long sought to keep missionaries out of its territories lest the antagonism aroused by their efforts bring unrest and jeopardize trade.

In this period migrations of professedly Christian peoples had a more important share than before in the spread of Christianity. The previous expansion through migration

had been confined chiefly to merchants, to the Syrian
Christians in South India (for these seem to have had their
origin in mercantile communities), to the northward movement of Russians, to the Scandinavian settlement of
Greenland, to the northward and eastward movement of
the Germans, and to the crusades. Now Spaniards conquered a large portion of the Americas, including the West
Indies and the Philippines, and became the ruling classes
in these lands; the Portuguese established themselves in a
similar position in Brazil and sprinkled themselves along
the coasts of Africa and here and there on the shores of
India, in the East Indies, and in Malacca and Macao; the
French planted colonies in parts of North America and
the West Indies; the Dutch, with an intermingling of
French Huguenots, began a permanent colony in South
Africa, and Dutch groups, largely of merchants and
officials, were found in various places in the East Indies,
India, Ceylon, and the Americas; the British obtained
possession of some of the West Indies and there became
officials and owners of plantations; and in the English
colonies in North America immigrants, largely Protestant,
from several nations began what in time was the numerically largest overseas population of European descent. The
retention of their hereditary faith by these peoples was
presumptive but neither inevitable not automatic. When,
as in America, Europeans erased the antecedent cultures,
the persistence of Christianity among the immigrants was
probable. In Asia, however, among peoples of high
civilization, it would not have been surprising if Europeans
had taken on the faiths of the lands in which they settled.
In British North America many for a time tended to drift
away from all religious faith. In general, however, in all
parts of the world those of European descent retained the
name of Christian.

As in earlier periods, the Church was a leading instrument in the spread of Christianity and in the conservation
of the faith in areas in which it had been planted. It was
the Church through which the influence of Jesus was
chiefly continued in Europe. When the Protestants broke
away from the Roman Catholic Church they did not

abandon the idea of the Church. Each Protestant movement, even some of the most radical, such as the Quakers,
centred its life about what was in fact, although not always
in name, a church. The very insistence of each Protestant
sect that theirs was the true church was evidence of how
closely the Church in some form had come to be associated
with Christianity. When absolutist states endeavoured to
propagate Christianity among their non-Christian subjects,
they sought to set up an ecclesiastical organization for the
converts. Overseas settlers carried the Church with them
and established it in their new homes as the normal
channel for their religious life. Probably this position of
the Church was to be expected. Christianity had so early
given rise to the Church that the two were regarded as
inseparable.

As they had been since the sixth century, so in this
period monks or representatives of a modified monasticism were among the active agents for the spread of the
faith. The state might direct, control, and finance missions
to non-Christians, but for missionaries they had to look
mainly to monks and members of religious orders who had
volunteered for that service. This was true in the Russian
domains. It was also true of the Roman Catholic branch
of the faith. In the latter, the older forms of monasticism
now had little part in providing missionaries. The Benedictines and the various orders which had arisen out of
the Benedictines took almost no share in the propagation
of the faith in new areas and among new peoples. This
was in striking contrast with the progress of the faith in
the early Middle Ages. It was newer orders, notably
the Franciscans, the Dominicans, the Augustinians, the
Jesuits, and, to a less extent, the Theatines, from which
came most of the missionaries. Only a minority were from
the secular clergy, and most of this minority were members
of the Foreign Missionary Society of Paris, which had a
semi-monastic form of organization. The prominence of
the newer orders seems to have been due partly to a
tradition which made them more activistic and missionary
and less contemplative and centred on the life of their own
communities than were the older ones. It was also partly

because their form of organization was more adapted to sending men to new areas and to the comprehensive covering of districts and, sometimes, of entire countries. Always, however, as heretofore, members of religious orders were supposedly more fully committed to Jesus and to the Christian faith than were the rank and file of the laity or even of the secular clergy.

Having rejected monasticism, Protestants were deprived of that traditional means for the propagation of Christianity. Yet, wherever in their commerce, conquests, and settlements they came into contact with non-Christian peoples they developed agencies for spreading their form of the faith. Usually the missionaries were clergy. Some of them were supported by voluntary societies created for that purpose. Here again, as in the case of the monk-missionaries of the Roman Catholic and Eastern Churches, it was chiefly those who were most earnestly devoted to the faith who offered themselves as missionaries and gave to the support of the societies.

Between A.D. 1500 and A.D. 1750 Protestants had a much smaller share in the expansion of Christianity among non-Christian peoples than did Roman Catholics. In the main this was because the leading conquerors and builders of the colonial empires of the day were not Protestants but Roman Catholics. It was not the absence of monasticism or a lack of zeal which accounted for the difference.

The control and support of the spread of the faith by the state which so characterized this era seem to have been at least in part responsible for a singular and significant phenomenon. In areas where the state or a commercial company had the direction, the resulting Christianity was largely passive. It gave rise to almost no new orders or congregations. It gave birth to very few movements either for the further spread of the faith or for attacking collective evils. Morally it usually fell further short of the ideals and commands of Jesus than did the Christianity of the mother country. This was true whether the form of Christianity propagated was Russian Orthodox, Roman Catholic, or Protestant. It was about equally characteristic of the Spanish, the Portuguese, the Russian, and the Dutch possessions—those in which the policy of autocratic control by the secular arm was most marked. Apparently, when shackled by the secular authorities and used as an arm of the state, neither the Church nor the zeal of the monks could instil the kind of life which would issue in spontaneous religious movements or efforts to bring society into conformity to Christian standards. The majority of the missionaries were European-born. Most of those who fought the enslavement and maltreatment of the indigenous peoples were natives of the mother country and not of the colonies. To be sure, these missionaries and reforms were from churches which in Europe were subject to the absolutist states of the period. Yet in Western Europe the traditional position of the Church had earlier been one of independence or semi-independence of the state. Apparently enough of this spirit carried over into the absolutist age to allow and encourage initiative. In colonial possessions, however, where from the first subservience to the secular arm had been the rule, the attitude of passivity was not offset by a heritage of freedom. Even in the nineteenth and twentieth centuries, when the subordination to the state was weakened, in the areas in which Christianity had been planted in the sixteenth, seventeenth, and eighteenth centuries under state direction, the lack of initiative continued. This was the case in Spanish and Portuguese America, in the remnants of Portuguese holdings in Asia, and in the state church in the Netherlands Indies. It was painfully apparent in Russia, where to the Byzantine tradition of the subjection of the Church to the state had been added the influence of Western European absolute monarchy, notably under Peter the Great. The Russian Church was tied hand and foot to the Crown. It was in the monasteries, where some elements of freedom continued, and among the sects which dissented from the state church that such spontaneity and inward vitality as persisted in Russian Christianity were chiefly apparent.

In striking contrast with the lack of initiative and the low morale of the Christianity of the lands in which the absolutist state had the Church under its full control was the abounding vigour which was beginning to be

displayed in the English colonies in North America. Here
Christianity was planted with very little assistance from
the government of the mother country. It was introduced
in part, as in New England and Pennsylvania, by groups
who were seeking haven from persecution on the other
side of the Atlantic and who on their own volition had
come to the New World and set up their churches. Here
and there it received assistance, notably in the case of the
Church of England and of missions to the Indians, from
societies voluntarily organized in the homeland. This aid
was chiefly financial. After the first generation the personnel was largely American-born. It is true that in the
majority of the Thirteen Colonies one form or another of
Christianity enjoyed the peculiar favour of the colonial
government. That was the case with the Congregational
churches in most of New England. In some others of the
colonies the Church of England was established. However, these special positions as against other groups were
not so persistently and strictly enforced as in most of contemporary Europe. In the Thirteen Colonies the tendency
was towards religious liberty. In some it was already very
marked. Full freedom of conscience and the complete
separation of Church and state were not achieved without
a struggle and did not come until after A.D. 1750. However, the trend was in that direction. We must also note
that the large majority of those who migrated from the
Old World to the Thirteen Colonies did so from other
than religious motives and that as late as A.D. 1800 less
than one-tenth of the population of what by then had
become the United States held membership in any of the
churches. The proportion of formal church members was,
therefore, much smaller than in Spanish and Portuguese
America. Yet the churches in the Thirteen Colonies displayed much greater vitality than those in any other of the
overseas possessions of Europe. They were largely self-
governing, with either complete independence or a minimum of direction from the churches of Europe. More and
more of their clergy was colonial-born rather than from
across the Atlantic. From them missionaries went out to
the Indians. In the first half of the eighteenth century

a religious movement, the Great Awakening, sprang up among them, with a leadership which was largely native-born and trained. This revival had profound and lasting effects and was without parallel in Spanish or Portuguese America. In the nineteenth century the vitality was to continue. The percentage of church membership in the population greatly increased. The Christianity of the United States not only spread to the Indians and to the much larger body of Negroes. It also took a growing share in propagating Christianity the world over. That share was much greater than that assumed by the Roman Catholic Church of Latin America, a Church which once had been far larger and wealthier.

The vigour in the churches in the Thirteen Colonies was not restricted to any one denomination. It was seen not only among Protestants, but also, before the close of the eighteenth century, in the very small Roman Catholic minority. Apparently the favouring condition was the freedom of the churches from state domination, as con-trasted with the subservience in which the Church was kept by the state in other European possessions.

This vigour of a church unhampered by the close even though friendly control by the state has parallels in the enormous spread of Christianity through the Church in the Roman Empire before Constantine, in the vitality of the Church in Western Europe during the Middle Ages, and in the phenomenal expansion of Christianity in the nineteenth and twentieth centuries from churches which were either independent of the state or were less tram-melled by it than had been most of the churches of the sixteenth, seventeenth, and eighteenth centuries. The vast expansion of the faith in these centuries unquestionably led to a healthier and more hardy Christianity in areas where state direction was the least marked and where indigenous leadership prevailed.

CHAPTER VI: THE THIRD MAJOR RECESSION

A.D. 1750—A.D. 1815

In the eighteenth century came a new recession in the Christian tide. It was neither so prolonged nor so severe as its two predecessors. While the boundary dates, A.D. 1750 and A.D. 1815, are only approximate, it is clear that the period was very much shorter than the other two. Like the other two, it was marked by losses of territory and threats to the continuation of the faith in the chief centres in which the influence of Jesus was strongest.

The actual losses in territory were not great. In Japan the persecution which had commenced late in the sixteenth became more acute in the seventeenth century. The Christians decreased and the survivors were forced to conceal their religion. In China the number of Christians, at best only a minority, remained about stationary in the eighteenth century and the morale of the Christian communities suffered. In Spanish and Portuguese America the rate of advance in winning the frontier slowed down. In Paraguay, once flourishing Christian communities broke up and disappeared. At the close of the eighteenth century and in the opening years of the nineteenth century many of the missions in Spanish America were discontinued. Some of them were turned over to the secular clergy, a step which was usually followed by deterioration. Some were transferred from one order to another or disappeared completely. In Russia here and there reversions to paganism occurred among tribes recently won to the state church. The heroic but futile efforts to establish Christianity in Tibet fell into abeyance. Christianity was introduced into Korea late in the eighteenth century only to meet with recurring persecutions.

The reasons for these territorial misfortunes were numerous and most of them were not interrelated. In part they were due to the decline of the two nations, Spain and Portugal, whose imperial expansion and zealous support had been so largely responsible for the spread of the faith beginning with the close of the fifteenth century. The reasons for that decay are obscure, but seem not to have arisen from anything inherent in the Christian faith which these peoples professed. Being stagnant, however, Spain and Portugal did not push missions as they had once done. In the second half of the eighteenth century the Society of Jesus, which had been a leader in the propagation of the Roman Catholic form of the faith, was expelled from the domains of Spain, Portugal, and France, the outstanding Roman Catholic colonial powers of the day, and therefore the ones through which most of the Roman Catholic contacts with non-Christian peoples had been made, and then was dissolved by the Pope. This proved a severe blow to missions in several regions. It was responsible for the collapse in Paraguay, where the Jesuits had been in charge, and contributed to the weakening of the Church in some other parts of Latin America and in China and India. In China persecutions had much to do with the stationary nature of the Christian community. These arose partly from the fact that the Manchu Dynasty, then ruling the Empire, was beginning to show the first signs of the disintegration which was to end it over a century later and, as one of these symptoms, was timorous of anything which carried the least flavour of rebellion. It was, therefore, suspicious of all secret or semi-secret religious groups and among these classified the Christians. Moreover, a prolonged and bitter controversy among the missionaries over the proper attitude towards some important Chinese customs, or rites, weakened the approach to the Chinese. Widespread scepticism which dealt severe blows to the Church in Europe undercut religious conviction and slowed down the propagation of the faith. This was associated with a rationalism which penetrated the Church itself. Partly as an outgrowth of this rationalism was the Deism which declared its belief in a universal "natural religion," the fruit of human insight and reason, and which decried as untenable the special revelation which was Christianity's claim to uniqueness. Rationalism affected both Protestantism and Roman Catholicism, and Deism originated in Protestant circles, but both made serious inroads upon Roman Catholicism, particularly in the strongest of the

Roman Catholic powers of the century, France. Then
came a series of wars and revolutions which upset the old
political and social order. The British drove the French
out of North America and so ended for a time the widely
scattered French missions among the Indians. The American Revolution was accompanied by a lowering of the
religious vitality of the nascent United States. It was not
until late in the 1790's and early in the 1800's that the
revivals again broke forth. On the continent of Europe
the French Revolution and the wars which accompanied
and followed it dealt the Church, and especially the
Roman Catholic Church, severe blows. For a time few
new Roman Catholic missionaries could be sent and little
financial support could be provided for those who were
already at work. On top of the American and French
Revolutions, and in part as an outgrowth of them and of
the Napoleonic Wars, came a series of revolutions which
disrupted the established order in Latin America, the area
in which the faith had had its largest geographic expansion
in the sixteenth, seventeenth, and eighteenth centuries.
As a result, the Roman Catholic Church was largely
deprived of its European-born leadership, many of the
frontier missions came to an end, and the difficult adjust-
ments to the governments which succeeded the colonial
régime weakened the Church. In some sections of Latin
America the Church became the strongest bulwark of the
old social and economic régime, a guardian of a disappearing society. It was in danger of perishing with the
old order with which it was associated. Even though that
danger did not fully materialize, weakness and decline in
morale overtook the Church in what had seemingly been
the scene of some of its greatest triumphs in the preceding
period. From this brief rehearsal it must be obvious that
no factor common to all underlay these various causes of
territorial loss.

In Europe itself Christianity met with reverses. The
morale of the Church did not sink to so low a level as in
the previous two eras of recession, but it suffered severely.
Rationalism brought a numbing of religious zeal. The
University of Halle, which had been a centre of Pietism

and of missionary impulse in Lutheranism, was captured by rationalism, at the cost of some of the limited Protestant enterprise for spreading the faith. The romanticism which was a reaction against cold rationalism did not always work a return to the Christian faith. Usually the sceptics continued a formal connection with one or another of the churches. However, in the extreme stage of the French Revolution there was open repudiation of Christianity. Many with whom the French Revolution was popular were inclined to scoff at Christianity as an outworn superstition from which man was to be freed in the new day. Napoleon Bonaparte, while retaining an outward allegiance to the Church, dealt most cavalierly with the Pope. The wars associated with his name were not conducive to warm religious life.

However, in this period of seeming decline, as in those before it, Christianity was putting forth new movements which in succeeding years were to issue in an unprecedented strengthening of the influence of Jesus. This was particularly apparent in Protestantism.

In the seventeenth century, shortly after the deep suffering and prolonged devastation wrought in Germany by the Thirty Years War, new vigour had appeared in German Protestantism and had taken the form of Pietism. Out of Pietism and refugee remnants which survived the near erasure of Protestantism in Bohemia and Moravia during the Thirty Years War came the Moravians. Although never a large group, in the first half of the eighteenth century the Moravians inaugurated missions in widely scattered sections of the globe and contributed to what was eventually the much more extensive Wesleyan movement. The revival associated with the name of John Wesley was growing in strength in the second half of the eighteenth century and was making a profound impression in the British Isles, the British West Indies, and the United States. The awakening in British Protestantism was much broader than Wesley and the Methodists. It was becoming apparent in some of the older Nonconformist bodies. In the Church of England it was represented by the Evangelicals, a strain which owed much to John Wesley but

was not solely the outcome of his labours. About the turn
of the century, revivals broke out in the United States,
especially along the frontier, and were the means of greatly
strengthening the Protestantism of that country and of
planting and reinforcing the faith in the new settlements
of the West and North.

Moreover, these years of revolutions and wars witnessed
the inception of so great an expansion of Protestant
Christianity that they are sometimes said, although in-
accurately, to mark the beginning of Protestant missions.
It was in 1792, when the French Revolution was upsetting
the monarchy in France and threatening the Roman
Catholic Church, that William Carey stimulated the
formation of the Baptist Missionary Society in England.
It was in the period of the French Revolution and the
Napoleonic Wars, when England was threatened by the
conflagration on the Continent, that such organizations as
the London Missionary Society, the Church Missionary
Society, and the British and Foreign Bible Society came
into being. In 1797, while Holland was under the French
heel, the Netherlands Missionary Society was formed. In
New England, when the economic life of that section was
suffering from the Napoleonic Wars and almost on the eve
of the Second War with Great Britain, the American Board
of Commissioners for Foreign Missions came into existence,
the oldest large society in the United States for foreign
missions. While that war with Great Britain was being
waged, the Baptists of the United States organized for the
conduct of foreign missions. When England was engaged
in her life-and-death struggle with Napoleon, Carey, now
in India, was proposing periodical interdenominational and
international gatherings for co-operative planning for the
world-wide preaching of the Christian Gospel. This dream
did not then come to fruition, but it anticipated by a
little more than a century the formation, shortly after
the next general European war, of the International
Missionary Council, which was to undertake this very
function.

Here, then, was further evidence of that vitality within
Christianity which so often has broken out in the darkest

days in unexpected places and later has carried the influence of Jesus to a new high-water mark.

Had we lived between A.D. 1750 and A.D. 1815, however, we might have had no such confident or cheerful picture of the future. Again an old order was passing in connection with which Christianity had enjoyed a great expansion. That particular stage of expansion had slowed down and in places had become a recession. It was from a wing of Christianity, Protestantism, which thus far had been fairly limited geographically and, with some exceptions, had not been especially active in propagating its faith among non-Christian peoples, that an advance was beginning which in the following period was to take on dimensions of unprecedented magnitude.

CHAPTER VII: THE FOURTH GREAT AGE OF ADVANCE

A.D. 1815—A.D. 1914

After the brief recession which marked the second half of the eighteenth and the first decade and a half of the nineteenth century there came a fresh advance in the influence of Jesus. Once more this influence surpassed its previous achievements in the extent of its geographic spread. Whether it exceeded them in its effect upon Western European peoples is not entirely clear. That it left a greater impress than ever before upon mankind as a whole seems incontestable.

Never had Christianity or, indeed, any other system or set of ideas been so widely spread as in the century which followed the close of the Napoleonic Wars. In the United States the proportion of the population which had membership in one or another of the churches greatly increased. This was in spite of a prodigious growth in population due partly to the excess of births over deaths and partly to immigration from Europe. Into the new communities which arose on the westward-moving frontier Christianity was built as an integral part of their lives. The vast majority of the immigrants and their descendants were held to their hereditary faith. About half of what had been the largest non-Christian element of the population, the Negroes, became professedly Christian. Approximately half of the Indians were won to a similar allegiance. The new nation which arose to the north of the United States, in British North America, while much smaller in population than its neighbour, had a larger percentage which claimed a church connection. In the British West Indies most of the Negroes who constituted so large a proportion of the population gave at least nominal allegiance to Christianity. In Latin America the losses suffered by the Roman Catholic Church in the revolutions which brought political independence were partly recouped. Here and there missions were resumed or inaugurated among the Indians on the frontiers of white settlements. Of the large immigration from Europe to the southern part of South

America many maintained their relations with the Church. Protestantism was firmly planted in several of the Latin American countries, in part by immigration from Europe and in part by missions. The latter were chiefly from the United States. In the smaller island groups of the Pacific, such as Hawaii and the Fijis, the majority of the native population became Christian. In Australia and New Zealand an extensive immigration from Europe brought new nations into existence which preserved the Christian faith of their ancestors. In the Netherlands Indies the number of Christians markedly increased. Christianity was reintroduced into Japan and rapidly gained adherents. In Korea it emerged from the stage of persecution into one of toleration, and flourished. In China the Christians multiplied, especially after A.D. 1900. In Indo-China and in Burma striking growth was registered. India saw a substantial rise in the numbers of Christians. Partly through migration and partly through conversion, Christian groups were scattered across Siberia. Immigration from Europe replanted Christianity in North Africa. Africa to the south of the Sahara was the scene of extensive additions to the Christian churches. In South Africa a new nation arose, dominated by a thriving white minority most of whom were at least nominally Christian. Among the Negroes in many sections rapidly growing Christian constituencies came into being. On Madagascar a remarkable movement brought thousands into the Church. Not even in the sixteenth, seventeenth, and eighteenth centuries had Christianity been so widely disseminated. By 1914 there were few peoples among whom it was not represented, and the records of the sayings and deeds of Jesus had been put into hundreds of tongues.

The influence of Jesus was, through this expansion, being felt more widely than ever before. It was affecting the life of mankind as in no previous time.

In Western Europe a double phenomenon was apparent. On the one hand a number larger than in any earlier age, except in the years in which Islam was in the first flush of its conquests, were abandoning Christianity. They might still, as a matter of social convention, be baptized as

children and even be confirmed. They might be married
in the church and buried from it. Yet apart from these
formal acts millions now had no active connection with the
Church. Thousands were openly hostile. Many of the
intellectuals believed Christianity untenable. Some de-
nounced it as an enemy of progress. Among the masses
millions were indifferent. The labourers in the manu-
facturing centres which arose around the new industries,
especially on the continent of Europe, tended to drift away
from the Church. As in other periods of transition,
Christianity was at first strongest in communities where the
old order with which it was associated through its previous
gains persisted. On the other hand, great revivals occurred
in both the Protestant and the Roman Catholic folds.
Those who remained loyal to the Church—and they were
legion—were, in general, more faithful in their attendance
upon its worship and more earnest in attempts to observe
the requirements of their faith than had been the rank and
file of church members at any time since the first three
centuries. The co-extensiveness of the Church and the
community at large which had been characteristic of
Christendom since about the fourth century had not
entirely passed. Christianity was still ostensibly the official
faith of most nations of Western Europe. However, a dis-
tinction was beginning to be drawn. In a number of
countries Church and state were separated. A line was
appearing between the Church and the world. Increasingly those who were followers of Jesus were such by
deliberate individual choice rather than by the tradition of
the people or the nation and were distinct from those who
were not. This contrast can easily be exaggerated, but the
trend was in that direction.

On the surface the defection of so many millions seemed
to indicate that Jesus was a waning factor among Western
European peoples. The life of the Occident appeared to
be in process of secularization.

However, the situation was not so simple. To be sure,
no great philosophies and theologies were developed comparable with those of the Middle Ages or of the Protestant
Reformation. Education was passing out of the hands of

the Church and millions were coming to maturity with little or no instruction in the Christian faith. Yet among both Protestants and Roman Catholics a larger number of new organizations were springing into being for the practice and propagation of the faith than in any preceding span of years of equal length. More new orders and congregations arose within Roman Catholicism than in any other century. The Pope exercised greater effective control over the Roman Catholic Church than he had ever done. Ultramontanism and the promulgation of Papal infallibility were but symptoms of this tendency. The Papacy was less a political institution than in the Middle Ages and the Renaissance, and was more nearly exclusively concerned with moral and spiritual leadership. In Protestantism many new denominations and hundreds of societies were born. Awakening after awakening stirred the rank and file of Protestant church membership. For the average Protestant, Christianity was less a political movement, an affair of the community and the state, and more a matter of individual experience and commitment than even at the height of the Reformation. Protestant women and laymen were active in winning their fellows to the Christian faith. They did not leave this task to a specialized profession but considered it an obligation of all Christians. By both Roman Catholics and Protestants, and especially by Protestants, efforts were being made to reach the young and to follow those who were moving into the urban districts and factory towns. The centres of nineteenth-century culture were by no means surrendered. Many of the intelligentsia were devout Christians. Indeed, remarkable student Christian movements arose, notably among Protestants. Many of the labourers in the newer industries were Christian. In Great Britain the official labour movement owed much in its early leadership to Christians and had a strongly Christian tinge. Roman Catholic labour organizations came into existence. Education was being placed under the control of the state and was becoming secularized, but on the frontiers of white settlement, especially in the United States, those moved by their Christian faith were founding most of the institutions of higher learning and were even responsible for much of the public school system. The first stages of education for the Negroes were inaugurated by earnest Christians, black and white. In the United States Roman Catholics, at no small sacrifice, were constructing a network of parochial and higher schools for the education of their children under Christian auspices. Even the scientific method which characterized the period and which to many appeared a threat to Christian faith owed a debt to the Christian thinkers of the Middle Ages who had built into the foundations of modern Europe a confidence in the order and dependability of nature.

The political democracy which was one of the outstanding features of the century sprang largely from Christian sources. The prevailing optimism of the period which dreamed of creating a perfect human society had in it elements of Christian origin. Many of the movements which sought to make that vision a reality and which attacked the chronic human ills had a Christian rootage. This was notably the case in the successful campaign against Negro slavery, in the many efforts, not so successful, to curb war and bring about international peace, in the Red Cross for ministering to the sufferers from war and from natural disasters, in the inauguration of the modern nursing profession, in the fight against the excessive use of alcohol, in the efforts to improve the care of prisoners and the insane, in the multiform endeavours, never before so numerous, to give larger opportunities to the underprivileged, and in some of the many programmes for the thorough reconstruction of society. It seems probable, although accurate measurements are impossible, that impulses issuing from Jesus were more potent in shaping Western European peoples, both in Europe and in their newer habitats in the Americas, Australasia, Asia, and Africa, than in any previous era.

Upon non-European peoples, taking them as a whole, Christianity unquestionably had a greater influence than heretofore. This was seen in the planting and strengthening of Christian churches. It was witnessed in the abolition of the African slave trade and of African slavery. It was apparent in the reduction of scores of languages to writing, more than until now had been given a written form by all other agencies combined. Among people after people, from the most numerous on the globe, the Chinese, to some of the smallest, the inauguration of modern education of the sort developed in the Occident was chiefly the work of missionaries and their converts. Modern medicine, with its relief of human suffering, was introduced to many nations and tribes, mainly by Christian missionaries. Famines were fought, both directly and by the indirect method of providing means for an increased food supply, by Christian missionaries and those trained by them. Christians instituted better care for the insane and for the blind and deaf. Christians were usually the pioneers in obtaining an improved status and better education for women and girls. Again and again Christian missionaries strove against the debauching of backward peoples by the sale of liquor and the introduction of firearms. Among some tribes, notably in the islands of the Pacific, missionaries led in the complete reorganization of the collective life to meet the new conditions brought by contact with Europeans. In Japan they were advisers to statesmen in the reconstruction of a nation suddenly reopened to the commerce and the ideas of the world. In China, Christian missionaries were forerunners of the delayed but inevitable adjustment of the Empire's culture to the invading Occident. It was a Chinese trained through them, Yung Wing, himself a Christian, who was responsible for the first large contingent of his fellow countrymen who went to the Occident as students. It was another Chinese educated by them, Sun Yat-sen, also a Christian, who became the leader in initiating for China a new and revolutionary form of government to take the place of the old when it crumbled before the impact of the West. From Christians came stirrings of hope and doors of opportunity for the outcastes of India. Never had the currents issuing from Jesus penetrated to so much of mankind.

The extensive diffusion of Christianity and the concomitant effect upon mankind were achieved through a number of processes and because of several factors. Some

7

of these, as in previous periods, were not altogether compatible with the standards of Jesus. Some were flatly contradictory to them. Others were neutral. Still others were in accord with them.

Obviously the great spread of Christianity was made possible by the prodigious expansion of European peoples which marked the nineteenth century. By migrations of traditionally Christian peoples and by commerce and conquest Occidentals penetrated almost the entire globe. Only a few small and remote tribes were left untouched. The cultures both of primitive tribes and of highly civilized nations were modified or revolutionized. Since these non-European cultures, when intact, had non-Christian religions as an integral ingredient, they had previously, if they had enjoyed any contact with Christianity, presented a solid front against it. With the weakening or disintegration of these cultures the resistance to Christianity was lowered. Christianity had the advantage of entering in association with the culture of the dominant Occident. To be sure, its affiliation with the aggressive West sometimes provoked antagonism and often led to a misunderstanding of its true nature. In general, however, much less opposition was encountered than formerly and a prestige accrued to the faith which was that of the victorious and wealthy West. To many Christianity seemed a possible key to the power which was the envy of non-Europeans and a vehicle by which the desired techniques of the Occident might be acquired by those who hoped through them to attain the position and the wealth which the West possessed. Many a child was sent to a mission school because that was the only place in which education of an Occidental type could be obtained. A medical missionary was called in to treat a case, not because he was a missionary but because he was the only representative of Western therapy. In admitting the Christian missionary from these motives, the inward meaning of the faith could easily be missed. However, the missionary, if he was genuinely Christian, might through the door thus opened convey something of the spirit and message of Jesus. Indeed, that repeatedly occurred.

It would be interesting to inquire how far the expansion of Europe was due to Christianity. It would, however, be futile. No possibility exists of exact measurement. It is conceivable that the daring, the imagination, and the perseverance which drove Europeans in search of unknown islands and continents and of the North and South Poles and to the tops of unscaled mountains had at least in part a Christian origin. Undoubtedly the hope for gain through commerce was potent in European expansion. So, too, was the desire for power and prestige and the dream of achievement. These were the motives, rather than those derived from Christianity, which were the more obvious. It was only occasionally, as in David Livingstone, that a purpose clearly of Christian provenance was dominant. That Christianity was one of the causes of the spread of European peoples is, however, clear.

The expansion both of Europe and of Christianity was facilitated by the new mechanical appliances and the mounting wealth associated with the Industrial Revolution. It was machines which produced the outpouring of goods whose sale sent Europeans to the ends of the earth. Machines speeded up transportation and communication and so reduced the size of the earth that it was possible for Europeans, including Christian missionaries, to cover it. The monopoly of the new machines enabled Westerners to gain the mastery of most of the earth's surface and to impose their will upon other peoples. From the machines was derived the wealth a portion of which, albeit a very small proportion, Occidentals devoted to the spread of their faith. It was the exhilaration of the power and the wealth made available and of the doors opened by the machine which accounted in part for that abounding optimism of the nineteenth century with which the spread of Christianity was so closely associated.

How far the mechanical inventions of the age were due to Christianity is also beyond accurate determination. That the confidence in an orderly universe and the impulse to venture on the unexplored which lay back of them, as of the science and the geographic expansion of the age, were to some extent from the Christian faith appears clear.

Yet whether Christianity was the major source would be difficult either to prove or to disprove.

In the nineteenth-century spread of Christianity armed force had much less share than in any age since Constantine. To be sure, force was employed to blow open doors heretofore closed to the European and to subjugate non-European peoples. Because of their monopoly of the new machines, however, no war attendant upon the European conquests of the period was so prolonged or so exhausting for either victor or vanquished as had been many others. Victory was usually quickly achieved. When barriers were blasted down, it was very infrequently for the purpose of protecting missionaries. The safety of missionaries was occasionally, as in the French conquests in Indo-China, made the excuse for imperialistic advance. Of the leading colonial powers France was most active in the support of missions. Yet the French governments which backed up Roman Catholic missionaries abroad were often anti-clerical at home. Their favour was purely for political purposes.

For the majority of missionaries special undergirding by their governments was lacking. The leading colonial power, Great Britain, subsidized the schools of missionaries in her possessions. She did this, however, not because they were Christian but because they were schools. The United States, from which came more Protestant missionaries than from any other land except the British Isles, as a government gave no especial aid to them abroad. Some assistance was accorded mission schools among the Indians within the borders of the country, but this, as in the case of the British, was because they were schools and not because they were connected with churches. Usually governments interested themselves in the personal safety of missionaries in foreign lands and insisted that these emissaries of the churches be given their rights under the treaties, but they did this as they would for any of their citizens, regardless of occupation. British officials often resented the presence of missionaries as presumably prejudicial to trade and were more grudging in backing the legal rights of this group than of the merchants.

In its spread, Christianity was given much smaller financial assistance by governments and was less under state control than in the preceding period. The Russian was the only government which continued in full the older tradition. It employed Christianity as an aid to the assimilation of non-Russian tribes. Yet Russian missions were numerically slight when compared with those of Protestants and Roman Catholics.

This decline in the use of force and of state control and financial aid was due in part to the growing separation of Church and state which characterized the nineteenth century.

The separation of Church and state arose from contradictory motives. On the one hand were religious scepticism and anticlericalism which sought to free the state from any control by the Church. On the other was a growing conviction among Christians that the Church was compromising itself and its message by an alliance with the state, which all too often meant control by civil officials who had little interest in seeing that the Church presented the Christian message in its purity. In some regions, as in the United States, Canada, and Australia, the separation was hastened by the objection of nonconforming churches to the establishment by the state of a particular denomination.

The lack of active support by the state was, however, chiefly from another feature of the expansion of Christianity in the nineteenth century, the very large participation of private enterprise. Never had so many societies arisen for the spread of Christianity. It was through these societies that the expansion of the faith was mainly achieved. Never had so large a proportion of the laity actively interested themselves in the propagation of the faith. In the first five centuries no extensive organization or considerable financial undergirding had been necessary for the spread of the Christian message. In the years between the fifth and the nineteenth century the vast majority of missionaries had been monks, professionally religious, and their financial support had come either from the labours of their own hands, from their converts, or from princes. In the nineteenth century, in contrast, millions of lay folk, both

Protestant and Roman Catholic, contributed to the associations which maintained missionaries. These millions were only a minority of the total membership of the churches, but in the aggregate their numbers were very impressive. In some Protestant bodies the entire denomination constituted itself a missionary society and the ideal was proclaimed that every member should aid in the spread of the faith. More nearly than ever before, the propagation of Christianity became a popular enterprise, the concern of the rank and file of the parish clergy and of the church membership. In Protestant circles especially plans were deliberately laid for giving an intelligible knowledge of the Christian message to every living human being, and efforts were made to enlist in the achievement of this goal all Protestant Christians.

The prominence of private enterprise in the spread of the faith was closely associated with outstanding features of the nineteenth century—private initiative in business, *laissez faire* economics with a minimum of government control and support, and the growth of democracy. The close of the eighteenth and the nineteenth century witnessed a reaction against the economic mercantilism and the political absolutism of the preceding period. In place of the close control of life by the state, and of commerce by the state and by huge chartered companies, came individual enterprise, the curtailment of the powers of monarchs, the establishment of republics, the growth of democratic institutions, and the reduction of the power of the state to as low a point as possible. This trend was particularly marked in Anglo-Saxon lands. It was from these countries that the propagation of Protestant Christianity especially proceeded, and it was Protestant Christianity which had the greatest expansion in the nineteenth century. In local and city governments in Anglo-Saxon lands control by the central administration was comparatively slight. The citizen took an active interest in local, county, provincial, and national affairs. Industry and commerce were through innumerable individuals, partnerships, and stock companies. As the century wore on, some of the stock companies attained a portentous size and smaller concerns tended to be absorbed in them.

As the century passed, moreover, government regulation of economic, intellectual, and social life increased. Yet in contrast with earlier periods the nineteenth century was marked by freedom for individual initiative and liberty of association for a great variety of undertakings. It is not surprising, therefore, that the surging new life in Protestantism and Roman Catholicism, and especially in Protestantism, found expression in multitudes of associations for the propagation of the faith. These came from both clergy and laity. In Roman Catholic circles they were required to have the approval of the hierarchy, but they usually began with humble folk and frequently with laymen and women. It is significant that the most prominent figure in the inception of the Society for the Propagation of the Faith, the leading organization formed in the nineteenth century for the collection of funds for Roman Catholic missions, was a woman, Pauline Jaricot, who was not even a nun. In Protestant Christianity, laymen, women, and clergy were often associated. Women formed hundreds of societies, local, regional, and national, to assist in the spread of the faith. Children, too, were organized to give to Christian missions.

The prominence of private enterprise in the propagation of Christianity in the nineteenth century was only a phase of the multiplicity of organizations privately formed to attack the evils of society and to promote the improvement of individuals and of society. Anti-slavery societies, temperance and total abstinence leagues, the state and national anti-saloon leagues, societies for the prevention of cruelty to animals, boards and associations for the support of libraries, hospitals, and the furtherance of education, peace societies, farmers' leagues for co-operative buying and selling, co-operative stores, Sunday schools, and Young Men's and Young Women's Christian Associations, are only a few of the many kinds of organizations which sprang up with the betterment of mankind as their objective. Some of these were avowedly Christian in purpose and origin. Many others, although not expressly Christian, were initiated by those whose impulse was clearly from their Christian faith and drew their support largely from those who were active members of churches. Many contributors and promoters of these organizations who had little or no connection with the churches and who might have repudiated conventional Christianity owed much of their purpose to contact with the Christian faith.

In the nineteenth century Protestantism was even more prolific in organizations than was Roman Catholicism. The privilege and duty of individual judgment which are of the essence of Protestantism, did not prevent co-operation. In Protestantism there was less tolerance than in the Roman Catholic Church of dictation by the heads of ecclesiastical hierarchies, and the Protestant spirit found congenial the *laissez faire* atmosphere of the nineteenth century with its relative freedom from state control.

This was particularly true of Anglo-Saxon Protestantism. The Lutheran Protestantism which was dominant on the continent of Europe by long tradition accorded more power to the state than did much of Anglo-Saxon Protestantism and limited the areas in which the Christian spirit might impel individuals, as Christians, to take the initiative.

Much more than in earlier periods, many of the organizations through which the influence of Jesus made its way into society had only a tenuous connection with the churches or were entirely independent of them. Except in Eastern Europe, the churches were now more closely organized and more nearly distinct from the society about them in lands where Christianity was the prevailing religion than at any time since the first three centuries. Yet more than at any other time the impulses derived from Jesus were being transmitted to society by voluntarily formed associations which had no organic connection with the churches.

This was probably because Christianity had so long been present that ideals of Christian origin had become a part of the cultural possession of Western Europeans, often without awareness of their provenance. It was also because the background of many of these societies was Protestant and Anglo-Saxon. In Anglo-Saxon Protestantism ecclesiastical divisions were more numerous than elsewhere. No one church included all in any one country who called themselves Christians, not even in the various portions of the British Isles, where state churches persisted. When Christians wished to join in an enterprise for the good of the entire community, nation, or world, they often did so in societies which were more inclusive than any one denomination.

One interesting result of this absence of an ecclesiastical connection of many of the bodies and institutions which historically owed their origin to Christianity was that numbers of them quickly became secularized. Earnest Christians brought them into being and saw them through the discouraging years of the struggle for existence. When they became better established they tended to pass into the control of those whose Christian faith was at best nominal and who might even disavow Christianity. Again and again this happened. to schools, colleges, universities, hospitals, libraries, societies for international peace, and organizations for social reform. It was usually only when a fairly close relation was retained with some one of the churches that a Christian purpose was clearly conserved.

Yet through these many organizations of Christian origin, even when they became secularized, Jesus was making Himself felt in human society. Often the connection with Him might seem to be lost and could be traced only by painstaking search into the history of a particular body or movement. Sometimes the ideals derived from Jesus became very attenuated and were partly or entirely nullified by tendencies which entered in the course of secularization. However, in general through them the influence of Jesus was spreading and was modifying human culture. The conformation to the standards of Jesus was never complete. At times the influence was very slight. At others it was marked.

As we have suggested, these extra-ecclesiastical movements for the alteration of society were particularly characteristic of Anglo-Saxon Protestantism. In Continental European Protestantism the transformation of society was not so prominent as an objective. Moreover, the churches were more closely controlled by the state than in Anglo-Saxon lands. The Roman Catholic hierarchy insisted, so far as it was able, on keeping under ecclesiastical control the various organizations to which the members of its flock belonged.

Among the non-Christian peoples to which Christianity was now carried, the Roman Catholics emphasized the building of the Church. Protestants, on the other hand, while planting churches, gave much attention to the transformation of the entire culture. They had, accordingly, more immediate effect upon a culture as a whole. In China, for instance, where Roman Catholics entered much earlier than Protestants and in 1914 were several times more numerous, they had much less effect upon the country. Whether for the far future Roman Catholics had acted more wisely than Protestants still remains to be seen. So far as past experience goes to show, the influence of Jesus is perpetuated through some kind of continuing community of Christians, one which is avowedly and specifically Christian. That is, it goes on only through what in the broad sense of that term is a church. Even when an organization is formed because of an impulse derived ultimately from Jesus but is not primarily intended to be a company of His followers, it tends rather quickly to be secularized and to lose His spirit and so to cease to be a channel through which He can continue to have an effect on mankind. Presumably wherever such enduring Christian communities are not founded, Christianity will wane. However, for at least the period between A.D. 1815 and A.D. 1914, Protestant Christianity, giving rise through its churches to movements for the transformation of society which often had little organic connection with the Church, was having a wider effect in mediating the influence of Jesus to the world than was Roman Catholic Christianity.

Protestant Christianity, indeed, had a much larger place in shaping mankind as a whole than at any time since its origin. From the standpoint of the history of Christianity, the nineteenth century was the Protestant century. This pre-eminence was both in the geographic spread of Chtistianity and in the shaping of human culture.

The relative prominence of Protestant Christianity was obviously due at least partly to two factors, the leading place which predominantly Protestant peoples had in the expansion of Europe and in the invention and development of the mechanical appliances which characterized the age, and the association of Protestantism with the democracy and the private enterprise which marked the period.

In the sixteenth, seventeenth, and eighteenth centuries the European powers with the largest overseas possessions had been Roman Catholic Spain and Portugal. Roman Catholicism had, therefore, the major share in the spread of the faith. In the nineteenth century the outstanding colonial empire was built by Great Britain, which was predominantly Protestant. Notable, too, for its rapid growth in territory, population, and wealth was a nation which had begun as part of the British Empire, the United States, in which Protestantism was also on the ascendancy. Great Britain owed her prominence in no small measure to the fact that the Industrial Revolution originated within her borders and that she long held the leadership in the mechanical appliances and industrial organization of the new age. The United States enjoyed its rapid growth partly because it early introduced the new machines and utilized them on an enormous scale in the development of its virgin resources. The commerce of Great Britain grew apace and London became the largest city and the financial capital of the world. The domestic commerce of the United States also displayed a phenomenal development and the wealth of the country mounted as though its people had possession of Aladdin's lamp. When these two nations were so prominent it was natural that the Protestantism which was part of their culture also expanded. The exuberance which characterized the economic and political life of these countries was also seen in their religious life.

In general, although not exclusively, British Protestant missions were in British possessions or in lands, such as China, which had been forced open to Western commerce by the British. The chief expansion of the Protestantism of the United States was within the rapidly growing borders of that country. Overseas it was largely, although by no means entirely, in lands in which British missions, from related Protestant denominations, were active; in islands, the Philippines and Puerto Rico, which had come under the flag of the United States; in Japan, which the United States had led in opening to the outside world; in Hawaii, with which the commerce of the United States had provided contacts and in Latin America, where geographic propinquity and the common possession of alleged republican institutions had nourished in the people of the United States an emotional interest.

Protestantism, and especially Anglo-Saxon Protestantism, had strong kinship with the democracy and the individual enterprise of the nineteenth century. It flourished in that atmosphere. It was in Anglo-Saxon Protestantism, as we have suggested, that the majority of the organizations for the spread of Christianity and the reform of society had their origin. The voluntary gifts of Anglo-Saxon Protestants provided most of the funds with which they were supported. Leadership came largely from Great Britain and the United States. It was significant that the language of most of the Protestant international missionary gatherings was English.

The important question arises as to whether this prominence of Anglo-Saxon Protestantism was because of the economic and political position of Great Britain and the United States or whether the latter was due to the particular type of Protestantism which prevailed in these lands. Or were both the product of some other factor or factors? Geographic position and natural resources certainly accounted in some degree for the hegemony of Great Britain. Nearness to the continent of Europe and yet a separation which permitted partial isolation from Europe's wars proved of enormous advantage. The possession of coal and iron, important minerals in nineteenth-century industry, was undoubtedly an asset. Race may have played a role, mixed though the human composition of the British Islands was. It seems an indolent evasion of basic problems to say that we do not know the answer to the questions with which this paragraph opened. The problem is unquestionably basic. Unfortunately it is also as yet insoluble. It has been said that capitalism, of which Great Britain and the United States were the outstanding representatives, is to a large degree a product of Calvinism, and Calvinism was an important ingredient of nineteenth-century Anglo-Saxon Protestantism. Yet the causal connection between Calvinism and capitalism is challenged and is, to say the least, highly doubtful. It is clear that Anglo-Saxon Protestantism made a marked contribution to the political democracy and the responsible individualism of the nineteenth-century Great Britain and United States. It shared in their birth and modified their development. The sturdy sense of public and private duty, the benevolence, the conviction of responsibility for the welfare of subject peoples, and the attitude towards wealth as a public trust, which were so marked, clearly had roots in the type of Protestantism which prevailed among Anglo-Saxon peoples. Whether, however, without this Protestantism democracy and individualism would have come into being, although in somewhat different form, and whether Great Britain and the United States would have been so prominent in nineteenth-century empire building we do not and probably cannot know.

During most of the nineteenth century the French took the lead in Roman Catholic missions among non-European peoples. It was in France that the chief societies for the collection of funds for Roman Catholic missions began. More Roman Catholic missionaries to non-Christian peoples came from France than from any other one country. This was in spite of the fact that during the latter half of the century there was a growing defection in France from the Roman Catholic Church. Of the traditionally Roman Catholic powers, France led in acquiring an overseas empire in the nineteenth century. Between this prominence of the French in Roman Catholic missions and the building of the French colonial empire a connection undoubtedly existed. Some of the energy which displayed itself in acquiring the political and economic empire also found a channel in the creation of an ecclesiastical empire. The French Government, as we have said, gave active support to French missions.

Perhaps in the parallel between the relation of the spread of Protestantism to the growth of the British Empire and of the United States, and of Roman Catholic missions among non-Europeans to the construction of the French colonial empire, lies in part the answer to our problem. The consciousness that an empire was in building stimulated earnest Christians to take advantage of the situation to spread the faith and gave them open doors for their endeavours. The growing wealth acquired by industry and commerce provided means for the support of missions. Yet but for strong religious conviction open doors would not have been entered and money would not have been contributed.

That the combination of imperialism and religious energy was important in the nineteenth-century spread of Christianity is borne out by the record in the smaller colonial empires. In the extensive remnants of the Portuguese holdings of previous centuries Roman Catholic missions were predominant, but the clergy from somnolent Portugal were not so energetic as those from vigorous France. In the Dutch possessions, especially in the East Indies, the majority of missionaries were Dutch, and of these the majority were Protestant, with a growing minority from the mounting Roman Catholic population of the Netherlands. They proved resourceful and active, as was to be expected from the vitality in Holland. Until late in the century Germany was without colonies, but the abounding life in the country found partial outlet in Protestant and Roman Catholic missions, largely in the British and Dutch territories and in China and the Near East.

However, as we have said earlier, the Christian missions of the nineteenth century, although often associated closely with commercial and political imperialism, were to a lesser degree tools of that imperialism than in the sixteenth, seventeenth, and eighteenth centuries, and even than in the Middle Ages. They were not so much employed as instruments of the secular arm as they had been by the princes of the period of recession which preceded the Middle Ages. The growing separation of Church and state was being paralleled by a declining utilization of the Christian faith as a reinforcement of the secular ambition of the political authorities.

Women took an important place in the spread of the faith and in the application of the principles of Christianity to current problems. In earlier centuries they had had little active part in the propagation of Christianity among non-Christian peoples. To no small degree this had been because the physical dangers and hardships incident to the career of a missionary ruled them out. In the nineteenth century they constituted an increasing proportion of the missionary staff of the Roman Catholic and Protestant enterprises and had a large share in raising the funds for the support of missions. Their participation reflected on the one hand the growing peace and order which characterized the latter part of the century before A.D. 1914 and the added ease of travel and on the other the emancipation of women in the Occident and their entrance into activities and professions formerly reserved for men.

The circulation of the Bible, especially of the New Testament, had an augmented role in the spread of Christianity, and particularly of Protestant Christianity. For this the Protestant emphasis upon the reading of the Bible by laity and clergy was partly responsible. The multiplied use of the printed page made possible by the machine contributed to it. The circulation of the standard accounts of his life and teachings among both Christians and non-Christians helped to make Jesus vivid to more millions than ever before.

Among all these agencies and factors which in the nineteenth century contributed to the extension of Christianity and of the influence of Jesus in the affairs of mankind, as heretofore, the Church had the central place. It is true that more of the organizations and movements which multiplied the impact of Christianity had a merely tenuous connection with the Church than in previous ages. Yet it was through the Church in one or another of its many forms that the continuing current of Christian life found its main channel.

Moreover, it was the abounding life within Christianity which was chiefly responsible for the remarkable and growing effect of the faith upon mankind. That life was favoured by a number of factors, some of them only

remotely connected with it.   Often it ran counter to some
of the most powerful forces of the century.   As in previous
centuries it was this inner vitality which was the outstanding cause of the persistence and spread of the influence
of Jesus.

It must be noted, however, that in A.D. 1914 Christianity
was still primarily identified with European peoples.   It
had been planted widely.   There were few nations or tribes
among whom it did not possess contingents.   Yet among
non-European peoples—except the dwindling remnants of
Eastern Churches in the Moslem Near East—the leadership
of the Christian communities was still chiefly of European
stock and the financial undergirding was primarily from
Christians of European blood in Europe, America, and, to
a less extent, Australasia.   Christianity had been scattered
around the world, but, except for a few remnants of old
churches in the Near East and India, it is doubtful whether
it had yet taken firm root among any non-European people.

CHAPTER VIII: THE LATEST AGE

A.D. 1914 TO THE PRESENT

Beginning with A.D. 1914, what may prove to be another major recession in the Christian tide came upon the world. Many would declare unequivocally that a major recession is upon us. Some would have us believe that Christianity is suffering the greatest reverse in its history, and that the ebb is eliminating the influence of Jesus from human affairs. That, however, is too early and too rash a verdict. Unquestionably the nineteenth-century world with which the remarkable expansion of the faith was closely associated is largely gone. Many of the factors which made for the extension of Christianity, both geographically and in its effect on civilization, have passed or are passing. Mankind has entered into a very different climate of opinion. Yet in these years Christianity, while retreating on some fronts, has advanced on others. In some respects, incredible though the affirmation may seem, it is more potent in the life of mankind than ever before.

It is as yet too early to make more than tentative appraisals of the era which was ushered in by the assassination at Serajevo in the fateful A.D. 1914. What is sometimes called, although not with entire accuracy, the First World War, was followed by a peace, now more correctly seen as an uneasy truce, in which much of the familiar nineteenth century persisted. Indeed, that war seemed to be a victory for the ideals and forces which had characterized the nineteenth century. Democracy appeared triumphant and to be effecting, in the League of Nations, the beginning of a structure for world organization. The nations which had been the great nineteenth-century exponents of democracy, and whose empires had shown the largest territorial growth in that era, Great Britain, the United States, and France, had won in the appeal to arms. Yet scarcely had the guns ceased firing when it began to be clear that the nineteenth century had passed. In the succeeding years that fact became increasingly clear. The European war which broke out in 1939, while bringing most startling developments, in general merely gave additional speed to changes already in progress. These changes have by no means come to an end. Whatever the outcome from a military standpoint of the wars now being fought, and whoever may be the victors, certain basic alterations have already been made in the civilization of the world. It might better be said that they are being made. We can now begin to see what they are, but they have not come to an end. Indeed, they seem only to be in their early stages. The era appears to be only at its inception.

Whether, then, we are watching the beginning of another major recession of Christianity we cannot now know. If it should prove to be a major recession, we cannot yet tell whether it will conform to the trend of the Christian tide thus far and be less severe than the one before it. To date, as we have seen, each ebb has been less pronounced than the preceding one and has been followed by an advance which has carried the faith forward to a new high-water mark in its effect upon mankind as a whole. We ought not confidently to predict that this will always be the case. Apparently that will depend partly upon the nature and strength of the forces which are working against the influence of Jesus and partly upon the continuing vitality within Christianity. Of the latter, the past record of Christianity enables us to speak confidently. Concerning the former it is too soon to be dogmatic. We must essay, however, a description of the trends so far as they have proceeded, make an estimate of the current situation, and, from the experience of the past, endeavour to forecast the future. For this last we must remember how few prophecies are literally fulfilled by the event. We must not venture to foretell details. We must content ourselves with broad generalizations. This forecast we will postpone to the final chapter. Here we will attempt merely an analysis of the post-1914 period as it has thus far been unfolded.

It is so obvious as to be a platitude that we are in a marked transition from one age to another. If, however, we are to assess the bearing of the change upon the outlook for Christianity, we must, at the risk of repeating well-known facts, seek to summarize the chief contrasts between the new and the old.

Those features in which the post-1914 differs from the pre-1914 world seem at first sight to indicate that Christianity is retreating.

In contrast with the relative peace which characterized the nineteenth century, especially the generation immediately before A.D. 1914, the years beginning with A.D. 1814 have been outstanding for their wars and threats of war. The present wars are proving more destructive to the old order and to existing institutions than was the War of 1914–18. The machines which in the nineteenth century were devoted chiefly to the creation of wealth have now been turned to the destruction of wealth. Between A.D. 1815 and A.D. 1914 no conflict that could be called a general European war broke out. Such wars as developed in Europe were brief and none involved more than four countries. Since A.D. 1914 we have had two general European wars and, since the possessions of Europe are scattered over the globe and mechanical appliances have tied mankind together, all the world has been profoundly affected. To these have been added an exhausting struggle between the two largest Far Eastern peoples.

These conflicts have unquestionably done damage to Christianity. They have disturbed the processes by which Christianity spreads. They have slowed down or disrupted communications between missionaries and the constituencies which support them. Some missionaries who are citizens of an enemy state have been expelled from the colonies of a belligerent or have been interned. Some have been called to the colours. In areas where actual fighting has occurred, notably in China, much of the regular work of the missionaries and of the churches has been suspended. In parts of Europe visited by the armies or threatened by them, normal church life has been disrupted. The attention and the funds of the philanthropically minded have been diverted from agencies for the spread of Christianity to the relief of the suffering brought by wars and to the spiritual and physical care of the fighting men and of prisoners. Moreover, war usually brings a sag in morals among the belligerents and deadens the life in the churches. Probably, although that is hard to measure, the wars since A.D. 1914 have worked harm in the morale of the Church as a whole.

With war has come the decline of the domination of Western peoples with which the nineteenth-century spread of Christianity was so intimately associated. To be sure, Western peoples control politically in square miles a larger proportion of the earth's surface than they did on the eve of A.D. 1914. Notable have been the British and French mandates acquired in the Near East as a result of the War of 1914–18, the extension of Russian influence in Outer Mongolia, and the Italian conquest of Ethiopia. Yet the prestige of the white man has suffered. The second largest body of non-European peoples, that of India, is loosening the bonds by which it has been tied to the British Empire; some of its spokesmen are demanding complete independence, and the British Government has already promised dominion status when once the present European war shall be over. Japan is enlarging her empire. Her "new order in Eastern Asia" threatens the position of the Westerner among the most numerous of non-European peoples, the Chinese, and in other portions of the Far East. Even before the recent Japanese expansion, China was curtailing the special privileges which in pre-1914 days Occidentals had won within her borders. The Philippines have been granted an autonomy which, if the procedure agreed upon is followed, will result in early full independence from the United States.

This freedom from the white man's yoke would have come had never a European war been fought. At least some and perhaps the majority of non-European peoples would inevitably have adopted the machines and the economic, political, and military devices by which the white man had obtained his mastery. By so doing they could eventually challenge the rule of the Occident. Indeed, the movement for emancipation had commenced before A.D. 1914 in the rise of Japan, in the successful opposition of Japan to Russia in A.D. 1904–05, and in the beginning of the Indian National Congress and the demands of the intellectuals in Bengal. However, it was hastened by the weakening of Europe through internal strife.

The waning prestige of the Westerner does not necessarily mean the demise of the Christianity which has been planted by him. It means, however, that the Christian message cannot count so much as formerly on its connection with Occidental culture to obtain a hearing. In India the rise of Hindus to power in the new governments has brought some curtailment of opportunities for employment by the state of members of the Christian minority. The leading exponent of Indian nationalism, Gandhi, objects to any activities by Christians which lead to the transfer of religious allegiance from non-Christian cults. The Japanese fear the Western missionary and the churches influenced by him in Korea and Manchukuo as possible centres of sedition, and have made life uncomfortable for them. In the portions of China occupied by Japanese, the missionary is under suspicion as a critic of Japan's aims and methods. In the long run, the weakening of the Occident may prove an advantage. It may free the Christian communities among non-Western peoples from their dependence on the white man and make them more self-reliant and self-propagating. This, however, can only be if the faith of these groups has sufficient inward vitality. In the test some may succumb.

A development which has been hastened by war has been the increased power of the state and the consequent curtailment of that individual and private initiative which was so striking in the nineteenth century and upon which the spread of Christianity and the impact of Jesus upon culture East and West were so dependent.

The heightening of the functions of the state had been under way before A.D. 1914. The movement towards socialism had been marked. The pendulum which had swung so far in the nineteenth century against the absolute monarchies of the sixteenth, seventeenth, and eighteenth centuries and the mercantilism of the eighteenth century had now begun a swing back which in some lands gave the state more extensive functions than it had ever possessed. Even in Great Britain, the great exponent of *laissez faire* and private enterprise, such steps as the adoption of state pensions for the aged and the dole for the unemployed had heralded the approaching end of the old order. In the United States private corporations were being regulated and the state was entering upon extensive programmes for irrigation, the conservation of forests, and the further control of banking. On the continent of Europe government had proceeded far towards an all-inclusive assumption of the various activities of society and its control of the individual.

The War of 1914–18 and its aftermath greatly accelerated this trend. In Russia the Tsarist régime, a representative of the older absolute monarchies, was supplanted by a communist state which took a much more thoroughgoing direction of all phases of life than ever the old had done. In Italy Fascism, while preserving some of the outward forms of the pre-1914 monarchy, brought in a totalitarian government. In Germany the republic which succeeded the monarchy had strongly socialist tendencies and was in turn displaced by the totalitarian Nazis. In the United States the New Deal enhanced the national government, but was simply speeding up the trends which were already apparent in earlier administrations. In Spain Fascism fought socialism and communism. Its victory probably brought as much power to the state as would the triumph of its chief opponents. In both the totalitarian and the professedly democratic countries, preparation for war and war itself increased the functions of the state and worked more and more curtailment of the individual.

This growth of the power of the state has been a pronounced menace to Christianity. We have earlier seen that the faith has thrived most in lands and ages in which the Church has had the greatest freedom from governmental control. This was the case in the first three centuries when, in spite of persecution, the Church arose and developed a virile community life. It happened again in Western Europe after the fifth century when the weakening of the Roman Empire left the Church as the strongest comprehensive institution, the one under whose ægis the culture of Medieval Europe came into being. It was true once more in the nineteenth century. Where, as in the Byzantine Empire, in Russia, and in the Spanish and Portuguese colonial empires, the Church was curtailed and under the control of the state, Christianity tended to be anæmic or quietistic. This fate has seemed to be foreshadowed by the post-1914 augmentation of the state. In A.D. 1914 education was already largely in the hands of the state and civil marriage had become common. Since A.D. 1914 education has increasingly been taken out of the control of the churches. In totalitarian states efforts have been made to abolish the churches' organizations for youth and to replace them with those of the state or of the dominant party. In Italy a compromise has been effected which leaves some powers with the Church, but leading Fascists have declared that Christianity and Fascism are incompatible. In Russia the function of the Church has been confined to worship, and even this is regarded with unfriendly eye. In Japan and its domains the government insists that Christians as well as non-Christians do obeisance at state shrines. Some Christians have complied on the ground that the rites are officially declared to be non-religious and purely patriotic, but other Christians have unquiet consciences and in Korea the work of the Protestant missions has been largely disrupted. In the colonial possessions of totalitarian or near-totalitarian powers, religious liberty is either non-existent or greatly curtailed, in contrast with the relative toleration in the British and American empires. Even where the Church remains comparatively free, the prevailing atmosphere of expecting the government to assume what private enterprise formerly undertook has tended to discourage fresh effort.

Patriotism, or, to give it a less pleasant name, nationalism, has become a religion, a rival to Christianity which has back of it all the authority of the government. This trend has been most obvious in totalitarian states, where patriotism is reinforced by ideologies which are in part or in whole hostile to Christianity. Even in Great Britain and the United States, however, where lip-service is still paid to individual liberty, those who conscientiously feel that allegiance to God must lead them to refuse compliance with some of the demands of the state find their way hard.

The age-long conflict, at best at least latent and often

chronic, or acute, between Church and state, seems for the time to be going against the Church. In some ways the state is now more of a danger than it has ever been in what has traditionally been called Christendom. Appliances such as the telephone and the radio, and a school system from which the teaching of Christianity is excluded and the ideals of the nation and loyalty to them are stressed, give the state a more intimate access to all its citizens than at any previous time. There have been absolutisms before, but never have they possessed such mechanical facilities for enforcing their will. In what was once Christendom these are now fortified with ideologies which, as we have said, are in effect rival religions. The absolute monarchies of Europe of the sixteenth, seventeenth, and eighteenth centuries dominated the Church, but they were professedly Christian. They used the Church to reinforce their power, but they left to it many of its former functions, and so, while employing it as an instrument of government, honoured it and preserved it fairly intact. The present state takes from the Church many of its activities. The existing totalitarianism seeks not to perform certain functions through the Church, as did the absolute monarchies, but to take them entirely away from the Church. In some respects Christianity is confronted with a greater menace than in the tragic decades when the triumphant Arabs, champions of a new religion, Islam, were establishing governments in what had been professedly Christian areas and through the machinery of the state were slowly strangling the churches and eradicating Christianity. The Arabs and their successors, the Turks, were no more fanatically enforcers of Islam than are the members of the parties dominant in the totalitarian states of their peculiar ideologies. The totalitarian régimes are better equipped to make their will effective. The new type of state is as grave a threat as Christianity has ever faced.

With the rise of the totalitarian states has come the eclipse of democracy. Even the states which cling to democratic ideals are constrained to sacrifice some of their democratic methods to defend themselves against the others. The spokesmen of totalitarianism declare that they represent a forward step and that democracy is as outworn as feudalism. They point with scorn to the weaknesses of nineteenth-century political democracy, now become painfully apparent through long experimentation. The delays of parliamentary procedure, the endless party divisions and the rapidly shifting cabinets in continental European countries, the selfish grabbing of pressure groups, the slowness in coming to a common mind and common action are only some of the frailties at which the finger of scorn is levelled. To be sure, some of the Nazis declare that their programme is more truly democratic than the political and social structures of the professedly democratic peoples. However, they vigorously denounce the types of government which are usually termed democratic. Even in the democratic states voices have been heard insisting that democracy is passing. These have included some mature men who have been lifelong champions of democracy and liberalism. The peoples of democratic countries are ceasing to be sure of their own institutions.

In the nineteenth century, Protestantism, which had then been the most active and widely expanding form of Christianity, was intimately associated with democracy. The chief strongholds from which it had most of its spread, and in which the majority of the movements and organizations through which it affected civilization took their rise, were two of the leading democracies, Great Britain and the United States. Many of the Protestant denominations possessed democratically organized ecclesiastical structures. The decline of democracy would deal a serious blow to this Anglo-Saxon Protestantism.

Moreover, most of non-Anglo-Saxon Protestantism and Roman Catholicism, while generally not so close of kin to political democracy as has been Anglo-Saxon Protestantism, have enjoyed greater freedom in democratic lands than in the totalitarian type of state. Presumably, they, too, have suffered.

Beginning about A.D. 1931 with the successful challenge which Japan gave it in the creation of Manchukuo, the League of Nations weakened and eventually all but disintegrated. The League of Nations and the institutions and processes associated with it were the product of the nineteenth-century peace movement which was largely a fruit of Christianity, and especially of Anglo-Saxon Protestant Christianity. Since at least A.D. 1815 the peace movement had been formulating procedures for the settlement of international disputes without recourse to war and for the development of international government. With occasional reverses, through the nineteenth century steps towards this goal had progressively been taken. After A.D. 1918 the goal seemed to be much nearer attainment. By A.D. 1941 most of the structure on which such hopes had been pinned appeared to lie in ruins. Here seemed a major defeat for Christian idealism.

The weakening of the peace machinery of the world has been intimately connected with another development of the post-1914 world, the disintegration of what was once known as Christendom. European peoples have been sufficiently moulded by Christianity to have that faith as an active ingredient of their common culture. That culture has contained other elements, most of them inherited from the Græco-Roman world. The Church, however, was a vehicle by which they were chiefly transmitted. Out of the Christian impulse, although utilizing concepts derived from pre-Christian Rome and Greece, international law arose as a generally acknowledged set of customs for the regulation of intercourse between states. In the nineteenth century, in consequence of the expansion of European peoples, this was extended to non-Occidental nations and was at least nominally accepted by them as part of that Western culture which they were eager to take over to win their entrance into the fellowship of the dominant Western world. If this international law were to be observed, it must be based upon generally accepted ideals and moral principles and be part of a common culture. In the Occident the necessary foundation was provided by Christianity and legacies from Græco-Roman culture of which the agents of that faith had been the transmitters. In Europe the unity was never complete. Long before the twentieth century it had been repeatedly menaced. The religious scepticism of the nineteenth century threatened it. However, the most serious blow which this European Christendom has suffered has been the rise to power of totalitarian ideologies in the post-1914 era. Russia was the first major defection, with the triumph in it of a communism which denied in theory and practice the validity of much of Christian ethics. Whereas after A.D. 1815 a Tsar of Russia had proposed to his fellow monarchs of Europe that they govern their states and their relations with one another on the basis of Christian principles, after A.D. 1914 a régime came into power which seeks to extirpate Christianity and to which some of the leading Christian virtues are anathema. Somewhat less openly, similar developments have occurred in Fascist Italy and Nazi Germany. Japan, never so profoundly influenced by Christianity as Europe, has fallen in with the congenial trend in the totalitarian Western powers. None of these has openly and categorically repudiated international law, but by cutting themselves loose from the never fully accepted common Christian idealism they have rendered more difficult the building of a world order towards which, largely because of Christianity, a beginning has been made.

To these changes from the nineteenth-century world, with which the expansion of the influence of Jesus had been intimately connected, has been added a deterioration in economic conditions which has undercut the financial support of the churches and their missions. The wars of the period have impoverished Western nations, added to the burden of taxation, and disturbed the financial, commercial, and industrial structure of the world. In Germany, France, and Italy, the decline in the value of the standard unit of currency has brought embarrassment and even suffering. The rising costs of government as the state has taken over more and more functions and the mounting armaments have added to the tax load. The world-wide economic depression which began in A.D. 1929 was more severe than anything of its kind which the nineteenth century had known. Those in the middle and upper income groups from whom most of the funds came which supported the countless philanthropic and religious organizations through which the nineteenth century sought to extend and apply Christianity have felt acutely the pressure of the increased financial burdens. Incomes of hundreds of organizations have declined, and that in the face of rising costs. In the pre-1914 decades the growing wealth made possible fairly constantly expanding budgets for churches and missionary and other benevolent societies. Now sharp retrenchment has become common. Inflation and declining interest rates have reduced the value of the endowments which thousands of the privately organized societies and institutions have accumulated. Since a characteristic feature of the nineteenth-century spread of Christianity was its dependence on the gifts of many individuals rather than on the state, the effect of these altered economic conditions has been distressing.

What has amounted to a revolution in the climate of opinion has occurred. The nineteenth century was, in general, marked by abounding optimism. That, indeed, had been prominent even in the quarter of a century of war and revolution which preceded A.D. 1815. Now deep pessimism and despair have seized much of the human race. To be sure, in the new totalitarian states the governments officially profess optimism and seek to inculcate it among the masses. However, where anything approaching freedom of the Press has survived, the printed page shows much of cynicism, fear, and discouragement. Among common folk as well as those highly placed, and among both victors and vanquished, are uncertainty, apprehension, and a search for security. There is a loss of confidence in human reason. Especially in the totalitarian states free thought and speech, associated with trust in the unhampered human intellect, have been repressed, and propaganda and reiterated dogmatic assertions by political leaders are the order of the day. Discussion and open-minded investigation are scorned and persecuted. The churches and Christian enterprise have inevitably been affected. In Protestantism, by its nature more responsive to current trends than Roman Catholicism, the optimistic liberalism of the nineteenth century has been partly replaced by crisis theology, and the confidence in reason and the intellect as competent in matters of religion has tended to be ushered out by a belief that God is utterly different from man and man is so corrupted by sin that knowledge of God can come only by God's revelation of Himself. The hope that human society can be made better which inspired much of the Christian activity of the nineteenth century has given way in many Christian quarters to a despair of the world. In such a world and encompassed by these attitudes Christian folk have found difficulty in reaching out to new enterprises, and often have been less than half-hearted in supporting activities and organizations which their hopeful fathers brought into existence.

The religious scepticism born of the rationalism of the eighteenth and nineteenth centuries, which had been a chronic threat to Christianity, has continued, in many quarters in aggravated and even belligerent forms. The cynicism and pessimism of the day have added to it. Among both intelligentsia and the rank and file a decline in Christian faith has seemed to be in progress.

In this transition from the nineteenth century, Protestantism has suffered more than Roman Catholicism. Since the nineteenth century was pre-eminently the Protestant century and Protestant Christianity was intimately connected with many of the movements and peoples which were then dominant, the fading of that century and of its distinctive features has proved a more severe blow to Protestantism than to Roman Catholicism. Indeed, taken the world over, Roman Catholic Christianity probably has gone forward since A.D. 1914 more markedly than has Protestantism. This has been seen partly in the rapid growth of Roman Catholic missions in non-European lands. It has been due to a number of causes. The mounting strength of the Roman Catholic Church in the United States has been a large factor, and this in turn has been due to the faithful efforts in the nineteenth century which laid the foundations for that strength and to the rise to comfort, and here and there to affluence, of Roman Catholic emigrants and their children, who, coming poverty-stricken to America, have profited by the development of the virgin resources of the land. Probably, too, the reaction from democracy to totalitarianism favoured a church in which nineteenth-century ultra-montanism had augmented the power of the already absolute Pope. The distrust of individualism and of individual reason has led many to welcome the kind of external authority embodied in the Roman Catholic Church.

What has looked like extensive loss of territory has reduced the geographic boundaries of Christianity. Here not Protestantism or Roman Catholicism but the Eastern Churches have been the chief sufferers. The collapse of the Tsarist régime and its eventual replacement by the communist soviet rule dealt disastrous blows to all of the older religions in Russia. Displaying many of the features of a religion, communism has sought to eradicate its predecessors and rivals. Many churches have been closed and their pastors or priests killed or exiled. Those churches which have been allowed to continue are compelled to restrict their functions to worship. All religious instruction of the young and all social activities have been ruthlessly suppressed. The Orthodox Church, being the largest body, has been the main victim, but the various dissenting sects and the Lutherans seem proportionately to have been fully as badly reduced. In the portions of Poland and in the Baltic countries occupied by Russia in A.D. 1939 and 1940 the churches were vigorously dealt with. In Turkey during the War of 1914–18 massacres and deportations all but exterminated the Armenian Christian communities. Protestants also suffered. After the war the expulsion of the Greek population largely eliminated, except from Constantinople, the Greek Orthodox from the republic. The new nationalist régime forbids conversions and has placed such restrictions on Christian missions that they have been brought to a mere fraction of their former numerical strength, and those missionaries who remain have found it all but impossible to do specifically religious work. The War of 1914–18, too, decimated the small surviving remnants of the Nestorians. In Egypt the Coptic Church, on the stubborn defensive for more than a thousand years, has continued to lose members to Islam, sometimes at the rate of many hundreds a year. For a time in the 1920's in China anti-religious movements, fomented in part by communists and a feature of the nationalistic effort to eliminate the special privileges enjoyed by Westerners, slowed down the growth of the Church and actually decreased the membership of some of the Protestant groups. While Christianity has not been completely eliminated from any country, in some lands, notably Russia and Turkey, it has been severely weakened. By these developments Christianity has suffered in square miles greater territorial losses than in any other period.

If these discouraging features of the post-1914 years were the entire story the era would unquestionably be one of major recession of the Christian tide. The ebb would certainly be more pronounced than the one in the second half of the eighteenth century. In some respects the threats have been more serious than at any time since the disheartening four and a half centuries which followed A.D. 500.

Fortunately this is only the dark side of the picture. The shadows have been black enough, but there is also light. Indeed, the light has been so marked and in some respects so strengthened that, viewing mankind as a whole, the picture, while one of even more striking contrasts than in the nineteenth century, indicates a growth in the effect of Christianity and of the influence of Jesus.

The territorial losses, momentous at first glance, on closer examination prove not to be so serious. The Russian Orthodox Church had long been bound so closely to the state that it had become anæmic and in the nineteenth century had been losing its grip on the nation. It speaks volumes for the vitality of Christianity that even so handicapped and decadent a representative should be the only important institution of the old régime to survive the communist revolution. Christianity is by no means extinct in Russia. Just how strong it is, we of the outside world cannot know. It is clear, however, that hundreds of churches remain open and are served by priests and visited by the faithful in spite of all the pressure of prolonged anti-religious propaganda. Some reports seem to indicate an underground trend towards Christianity, both of the Orthodox Church and of the sects. In Turkey the Church has not disappeared, and a movement, small numerically but earnest, has set in among some of the younger Turks, which, while disavowing the designation of Christian, is intensely loyal to Jesus. In Nazi Germany the churches, although deprived of some of the means by which they gave religious training to their young, and faced with other restrictions, continue. New church buildings have been erected and others renovated, even in the war year, A.D. 1940. The numerically weak confessional elements in the Protestant churches have presented determined resistance to the efforts of the Nationalist Socialists at regimentation. For several years after the Nazis came into power the sale of the Bible exceeded that of "Mein Kampf."

In a number of areas the years since A.D. 1914 have witnessed a striking growth in the numerical strength of the churches. In the United States the increase both in numbers and in the percentage of the total population which had been one of the features of the preceding century has continued, and that in spite of participation in the War of 1914–18 and the backwash against religion and morality which usually accompanies and follows war. In Negro Africa, especially in Equatorial Africa, a rapid rise in the numbers of Christians has been recorded. The War of 1914–18 was followed by an acceleration of the penetration of Negro Africa by white culture and by the progressive disintegration of native cultures. As a concomitant has gone the acceptance of Christianity by many thousands. This would not have been, however, had not missionaries, both Roman Catholic and Protestant, been present. In the Belgian Congo the support of the government has aided the phenomenal growth of the Roman Catholics, but in other parts of Africa, where such resistance has not been so markedly accorded, increase has also been registered in both Protestant and Roman Catholic circles. In India numerical advance has been recorded. This has been especially striking in the Protestant churches and among the outcastes. Mass movements have carried tens of thousands of the under-privileged into the Christian fold. Much of this surge of the poor and uneducated towards the faith must be ascribed to a vaguely defined hope that from the Christian connection greater economic, educational, and social advantages will come to them and their children Where baptism has not been preceded or followed by careful instruction, the Christianity of the converts has been nominal and superficial in the extreme. Yet the move has been actuated by some glimmering of an understanding of the larger life which the Christian faith opens to men and women. Instruction has been given to thousands. In many of the converts the moral, spiritual, and material improvement wrought has been so evident that some from higher social strata, impressed, also have become Christians. In the Netherlands East Indies, Christian communities, both Protestant and Roman Catholic, have grown. In French Indo-China, long almost exclusively a Roman Catholic field, the church has continued to advance. In China, in spite of the storm and stress of civil and foreign war and of the anti-religious movement of the 1920's, the number of Christians has mounted. The increase has been most marked among Roman Catholics. They have been represented in China much longer than have Protestants and since 1914 have greatly augmented their missionary staff. They have been, too, less the objects of anti-Christian agitation. However, Protestants have also shown a growth, although not so striking a one. In the face of the Japanese invasion and partial occupation, accessions to the churches have continued. In Japan the churches have grown. In Iran some advance has been made. Here, rather remarkably, a few converts have been gathered from Islam, a very rare phenomenon under a Moslem government. Full statistics are lacking, but it may be that, taken the world over, the losses in nominal Christians in the years since A.D. 1914 have been larger than the additions. However, the losses have been chiefly in Russia, whereas the gains have been widely distributed and have been partly in lands where Christianity has heretofore been weak. When one views the entire globe geographically, Christianity is stronger in A.D. 1941 and in a better position to influence the human race than it was in A.D. 1914. In most non-Occidental lands, especially the more populous, Christians are still in the small minority. These minorities have, however, in general become very much larger in the years since the

outbreak of the War of 1914–18. Christianity is not so nearly
exclusively identified with the Occident as it was in A.D. 1914.

In leadership, even more striking progress has been
made in establishing Christianity as the possession of
non-European peoples. This is seen among both Roman
Catholics and Protestants. Among most of the peoples
where it is represented, the Roman Catholic Church is
going to great pains to train a native priesthood. This
effort has been meeting with signal success. Rome, too,
has been raising non-Europeans to the episcopate. This is
being done not only among civilized peoples such as the
Chinese, the Japanese, and the Indians, where presumably
it is possible to find those prepared by background for
leadership, but a beginning is also being made among the
Negroes of Africa. Never has the priesthood and episcopate
of the Roman Catholic Church been so nearly inclusive of
all races as it is in A.D. 1941. Lay brothers and sisters are
also being recruited more than ever from non-Occidental
folk. Protestants are likewise making rapid strides in
developing indigenous leadership among non-Europeans.
Clergy and bishops are being trained and appointed.
Administrative posts of many kinds, ecclesiastical, educational, and medical, have been transferred from Occidentals
to non-Occidentals. In both Roman Catholic and Protestant circles this devolution from the control by Occidentals to the indigenous Christians has been hastened
and here and there forced by the rising revolt against white
domination which is one of the characteristics of the age.
It would have been impossible, however, if there were not
Christians at hand who are competent to fill the posts. At
the meeting of the (Protestant) International Missionary
Council at Madras in A.D. 1938, among the regularly
appointed delegates non-Occidentals were practically as
numerous as Occidentals, the first time at one of these
world-wide Christian gatherings where this has been the
case. It was generally remarked by the Occidentals present
that the non-Occidentals were on the average fully as able
as those from the West, and that they were young, an
indication of what is to be expected from the oncoming
generation.

In other ways Christianity is being naturalized among non-Occidental peoples and cultures. Churches and chapels are being erected in styles which reflect indigenous traditions. Christian subjects are being painted according to non-Occidental traditions. Jesus, the Virgin Mary, and the apostles are being represented as Chinese, Japanese, Indians, and Negroes. Hymns have been written in native poetic forms and to fit native tunes. Some of this has been done by Occidentals or under their direction and is not spontaneous. Much of it, however, has been by non-Occidentals as a genuine expression of their Christian faith.

In the post-1914 propagation of Christianity among non-Occidentals Roman Catholics have in some respects been making more rapid progress than Protestants. For reasons which must be apparent from the first part of this chapter, Protestant Christianity has been more jeopardized by the conditions which are making the new age than has Roman Catholicism. The Protestant missionary force increased for about a decade after A.D. 1914 and then, because of the difficulty of obtaining financial support, became stationary and in some areas declined. The Roman Catholic missionary staff has increased and funds have been augmented. This has been due partly to the temper of post-1914 days, partly to the growing resources of the Roman Catholic Church in the United States, and partly to the extraordinarily able and devoted leadership at Rome in the Papal chair and in the Congregation for the Propagation of the Faith. Yet in growth in numbers of adherents in non-Occidental lands and in indigenous leadership, the advance of Protestant Christianity has been about as striking as that of Roman Catholic Christianity. In traditionally Roman Catholic populations, but where the morale of the Roman Catholic Church has been low, in Latin America and the Philippines, Protestantism has had an amazing growth. It has been introduced from the outside, largely from the United States, and has not been spontaneous, but it has been increasing in numbers and in indigenous leadership and has been attaining ecclesiastical independence of the churches which initiated it.

In another respect Protestant Christianity has been making rapid strides. It has been achieving a comprehensive world-wide fellowship, a fellowship into some of whose expressions the Eastern Churches are also beginning to be drawn. Steps in this direction had been taken before A.D. 1914. However, progress has been accelerated since that year. The International Missionary Council has come into being as a co-ordinating agency for the foreign missionary agencies of the Occident and for the "younger churches" which have arisen out of that missionary activity. As members of this Council, national and regional bodies have been formed. Those in the lands of the younger churches have brought together in the beginnings of national Protestant movements the disparate bodies founded by missionaries from the West. In addition to the International Missionary Council, the post-1914 years have seen the World Conference on Faith and Order and the Universal Christian Council of Life and Work. The former has drawn Christians together to understand through discussion the positions on which churches have traditionally divided and to attempt to find common ground. The latter has sought a common mind on problems of state and society. Out of these two bodies has come the World Council of Churches, now in process of formation. In what are known for brevity as Life and Work and Faith and Order, and in the World Council of Churches, not only those in the Protestant tradition but also Eastern and Old Catholic Churches are included. Roman Catholics would be welcomed, but the leaders of their Church feel that officially they cannot consistently be represented. Here is emerging a world-wide Christian fellowship which is more inclusive ecclesiastically than any which has ever before been developed. In addition to these ecumenical bodies, Protestant groups have also coalesced in less all-embracing but still world-wide organizations. Some of these antedated A.D. 1914. Some came into being after that year. The Sunday Schools, the Young Men's and Young Women's Christian Associations, the Christian Student Fellowships, and the Young People's Societies of Christian Endeavour are movements which transcend both national and denominational boundaries. The Anglicans, the Baptists, the Presbyterians, the Congregationalists, and the Lutherans are prominent among the denominations which have achieved more or less loosely knit world-wide fellowships. While the nations of the world have, in such tragic fashion, been pulling apart, the non-Roman Catholic Christians of the world have been coming together. The mechanical appliances which nineteenth- and twentieth-century man has constructed have made it necessary for its own welfare that mankind the world over co-operate. By misusing those appliances the nations have been plunging the world into internecine strife. In the face of that disaster non-Roman Catholic Christians are beginning to achieve a fellowship which, like the Roman Catholic Church, reaches across national barriers. It is doubtful whether it can at any early date be strong enough to end the wars which wrack mankind. It can, however, ease tensions, allay suffering, and keep alive the vision and the purpose of a better world order.

Upon the cultures of mankind Christianity in the post-1914 age has been having striking effects. Among non-European peoples the contributions to education, medicine, and the warfare against famine and poverty have been marked. In China the government, with much larger financial resources than the Christian missions and churches, has made progress in building a modern educational system which has been rapidly outstripping the Christian schools in numbers and equipment. In medical training, too, state enterprise has begun to surpass in extent what was begun by the Christian missions. However, some of the best of the secondary and higher schools in China are still those under Christian auspices, and the best medical school in the country has been built on the foundations laid by Christian missions and has been financed by American Christian philanthropy. In an effort to remove the causes of famine, the outstanding pioneer school of forestry and agriculture in China has been developed in connection with a Christian university. In the Near East, Christian colleges and universities have been making a notable contribution in education. Among the majority of primitive

peoples, notably in Africa and the islands of the Pacific
the major part of the modern schools which have been
giving preparation for life in the ever-encroaching white
man's world have been under Christian auspices. Missionaries are still reducing languages to writing and preparing
the beginnings of a literature in them. The Bible is being
put into more and more tongues, and in many areas its
circulation has been increasing. In these aspects of culture
the contribution of Christianity has been chiefly that of
pioneering. It has stimulated the creation of a large
proportion of the earliest schools and hospitals, and has
initiated efforts to develop better methods of agriculture
and to introduce new grains and fruits. When the value
of the innovations has been demonstrated and governments
and non-Christian private agencies have become enthusi-
astic in adopting the new methods, the professedly
Christian institutions usually become less prominent.
Several of them still, however, with their freedom of
experimentation make fresh contributions.

Upon the collective life of some of the largest of the
non-European nations Christianity has increased in its
effects. In India the outstanding figure of these years has
unquestionably been Gandhi. Gandhi makes no profession
of being a Christian. Yet he has been profoundly affected
by his contacts with earnest Christians, both in the South
African stage of his career when he was developing his
methods and later in India itself. He counts the New
Testament and especially the Sermon on the Mount as
among the decisive influences upon his life. Through him
Christianity has had an effect upon all India. The more
active connotation given in practice to *ahimsa*, so widely
appealed to in the Indian nationalist movement, adding
to the older idea of passive harmlessness and non-injury to
any living being that of positive self-sacrifice, seems to have
come from contact with Christianity. The vast movements
among the outcastes of India, with the demands for the
lightening of their age-long disabilities, while reaching far
outside the Christian communities, have undoubtedly been
accelerated and possibly have had as a major source the
ideals and hopes which have issued from Christianity. In

China much of the most substantial and outstanding leadership in the unprecedented revolution and transition which have marked the life of the nation in these decades has been from the small Christian minority, and especially from the even smaller Protestant minority. The two most prominent and influential Chinese of these years, Sun Yat-sen and Chiang Kai-shek, have been convinced Christians, the former from his boyhood, the latter after his rise to power. More than any other one man Sun Yat-sen moulded the ideals of the new China. By his courage and faith Chiang Kai-shek has been the chief organizer of Chinese political unity and of resistance to the Japanese invasion. Other Chinese Christians, although less prominent, have stood out in government and in education as more dependable, more enduring, and more public-spirited than most of their non-Christian colleagues. Through the New Life Movement and other agencies, not specifically Christian, but deeply indebted to Christianity, that faith has helped to modify the lives of millions of Chinese who have not been even nominally Christian.

In the War of 1914–18 Christianity, especially the Protestantism of the United States, gave rise to efforts of unprecedented magnitude to relieve the sufferings which accompanied that struggle. Care for prisoners of war, relief for those threatened by starvation, and Near East relief usually had at their head those who were motivated by their Christian faith and for the vast sums which maintained them depended chiefly on the free gifts of Christian folk.

Thus far in the wars of the past four years, relief enterprises have not attained the magnitude of those of the earlier war. The reasons for the disparity are not altogether clear. They may be in part a weakening of the Christian impulse of helplessness and a discouragement symptomatic of the pessimism of the age and so may indicate a deepening of the recession of the Christian tide.

The creation and the later near collapse of the League of Nations may have a similar meaning. The League of Nations, as we have suggested, was largely an achievement of Christian idealism. It represented a high-water mark in the effort for the peaceful and orderly regulation of relations between nations. Its tragic fate has undoubtedly been a reverse for Christianity, and especially for nineteenth-century Anglo-Saxon Protestant Christianity.

Less prominent than the League of Nations, but issuing more clearly from Christianity, has been the Institute of Pacific Relations, an unofficial body for the study of the problems of the Pacific, with the purpose of bringing the leading minds of all the nations involved to bear upon their peaceful solution.

Chiefly out of Protestant Christianity came the prohibition of the manufacture and sale of alcoholic beverages in the United States, a movement which began in the nineteenth century but culminated after A.D. 1914 in national action. The repeal of national prohibition in the nineteen-thirties was a defeat for that branch of the Christian faith.

Aside from the relief enterprises of the War of 1914–18 and the League of Nations, the most striking fresh effects of Christianity upon the life of the race since A.D. 1914 have not been among Occidental peoples, where the faith has been longest present in strength, but among non-Occidental nations and races. Here have been the largest proportionate numerical gains. Here have been the most marked increases in shaping culture and political life. These effects, too, have mounted as time has passed. In the Occident they have suffered major reverses.

However, before coming too quickly to what might seem the logical deduction, that Christianity is a waning force in the Occident, we need to remind ourselves that in the Occident the Christian faith still bears some of its most characteristic fruits. It has continued to modify and radically to change individual lives. It has nourished faith, hope, love, patience, inward joy, forthgoing kindness, forbearance, forgiveness of injuries, and self-control. It has supported charities, small and large. It has been at the heart of care for the weak, the unfortunate, and the sick. These results cannot be measured in any such fashion as to permit of accurate comparison between the pre-1914 and the post-1914 world.

We must recall, too, that in the Occident Christianity has contributed to some of the major social and political revolutions of the time. Russian communism is pronouncedly anti-Christian, but historically some of the dominant features of communism are derived in part from Christianity. The belief so prominent in Marxism that human history is governed by law and culminates almost automatically in the victory of the exploited majority over the exploiting minority seems indebted to the Jewish-Christian conception of history. Back of the New Deal's professed concern for the "forgotten man" is to no small degree an attitude issuing from Christianity. As so often in the past, Christianity has contributed to movements which have been, as carried out, either contradictory to the principles of Jesus or have displayed some features which to him would be reprehensible.

In the methods by which Christianity spreads and by which it makes itself felt in civilization, the post-1914 years have not differed markedly from the nineteenth century. They have still been connected with the expansion of Western culture and with Western commerce and political imperialism. Governments have accorded even less support than before A.D. 1914, partly because the Tsarist régime which had so baldly used the Church to promote its ends has disappeared. Yet here and there, as in the Belgian Congo, the state has given pronounced aid, in this case through assistance to Roman Catholic education. Armed force has been almost entirely absent as a means of spread, except in so far as the police force has provided the kind of protection for missionaries that it would for the followers of any legitimate occupation. Private enterprise and support by gifts of thousands of individuals and by hundreds of organizations quite unconnected with the state are still the chief agencies both for the propagation of the faith and for seeking to make Christian precepts effective in society. Women constitute an increasing proportion of the staffs of foreign missionary enterprises. As in the nineteenth century, so since A.D. 1914, some of the most widespread effects of Christianity have been wrought through non-ecclesiastical agencies. Especially in Protestantism, the influence of Jesus has not been channelled entirely through the Church. New organizations and movements have appeared. What is known as Catholic Action has grown rapidly in many lands as a means of enlisting laymen in the promotion of the faith and in its application to life. What is variously called Buchmanism, from its founder, and the Oxford Groups, or simply the Groups, has had wide vogue in some Protestant circles. New Protestant denominations have arisen, although all of them are small. Within Protestantism the main trend is not towards the emergence of fresh denominations but towards the union of existing ones and towards co-operation.

This continuation of pre-1914 agencies and methods into the post-1914 age may be a symptom of recession. The seeming failure to produce new means to meet what is in so many respects a radically different world may indicate an ominous lack of resiliency. Yet we need to recall that in most of the world nineteenth-century conditions persisted into the 1930's, and that there has not yet been time for many new methods to emerge and become prominent. We must also remember that in producing non-Occidental leaders and in turning over to them more and more of the direction of the Christian movement in non-Western lands both Roman Catholic and Protestant Christianity have displayed imagination and adaptability. In the rapid growth of what is often called the Ecumenical Movement, non-Roman Catholic Christianity has been creating something quite new in Christian history and is seeking to counteract one of the most dangerous features of a perilous age, the political and ideological animosities which are dividing the human race.

Great, then, as is the menace to Christianity and strong as seems the evidence that the Christian tide is displaying a major recession, the counter evidence is by no means negligible. If there is a recession, it is not, when the world is viewed as a whole, as marked as the other three major retreats of the Christian movement. It is possible that we are at the beginning of one which will prove more extreme than some or perhaps any of its predecessors. That, however, is as yet not the case. To jump to the conclusion that it will become such is to take cowardly counsel of our fears. As a whole Christianity is displaying less weakness of morale and more vigour than in any of the three recessions which thus far have marked its course. Moreover, since A.D. 1914 Christianity has become more firmly rooted among more peoples than ever before in its history. While still having its chief hold, as it has since at least the tenth century, among peoples of Western European stock, in the past quarter of a century it has made striking progress among non-Occidental peoples not only in numerical strength but also in acquiring an able indigenous leadership and a growing independence of the tutelage of Occidental Christians. The Church is still divided, as it has been since its inception. No prospect is on the horizon of organizational reconciliation between the two most active wings, Protestantism and Roman Catholicism. Yet, in spite of its inherent fissiparousness, Protestantism is drawing together and is finding fellowship with some of the Eastern Churches. Striking gains are being registered which may later prove the basis of another advance of unprecedented potency. When the entire world is taken into consideration. Christianity is seen to have augmented its influence upon mankind.

CHAPTER IX: THE OUTLOOK FOR CHRISTIANITY

What is the outlook for Christianity? Is the influence of Jesus to wane or to grow? Even though we may be confident of the far future, what do the decades immediately ahead hold in store? Are the factors which threaten a recession to become stronger? Are we in the early stages of a momentous retreat, or are we on the eve of a fresh advance?

These questions are of major importance, not only for those who call themselves Christians, but also for the entire human race. Here has been and still is a major force in the history of mankind. No other set of ideas has been disseminated so widely. The dominant culture, that of the Occident, has especially been shaped by the Christian faith. If the influence of Jesus is receding and is progressively to decrease until it is eliminated, results will follow which will profoundly alter the entire face of human culture.

At first sight it would seem that the only wise reply is either silence or an evasive noncommittal. Unknown and unpredictable developments may nullify all our most careful calculations.

However, out of even so brief a survey of the record of Christianity as the past chapters have contained, certain generalizations emerge which provide a basis for confidence in some important predictions. We cannot hope to forecast details or even approximate dates, but conclusions as to main trends seem fully warranted.

It appears reasonably certain that Jesus will have a growing influence in the life of mankind. Ebbs in that influence may occur. They have done so in the past. There are some indications that we are now witnessing another ebb. Yet up to the present, taking the entire world into our view, that ebb, if ebb there be, is not so pronounced as any of its three major predecessors. Indeed, although it has not moved forward so rapidly as in the nineteenth century, since A.D. 1914 Christianity has grown in its influence upon the race as a whole. Whether the present powerful forces militating against Christianity will increase in strength and bring about a recession we do not know. However, in the past each ebb has been followed by a fresh advance and each advance has set a new high mark for the influence of Jesus in the total life of mankind. The presumption is that that in general will be the course in the future.

This presumption becomes as near a certainty as anything in the future of humanity can be when we recall that the appeal of Jesus has been proved to be universal. A century and a quarter ago we could not have been sure from observed experience that this is so. Then Christianity was still primarily the possession of European peoples. Even to-day it is chiefly identified with the Occident and its expansion is closely associated with that of Westerners and their culture. It is still largely dependent upon Occidental leadership and funds. However, Christianity has now been planted in practically every race and among the vast majority of the tribes and nations of the earth. While its entrance and acceptance have often been faciliated by the prestige of the culture with which it has chiefly been affiliated, it is clear that it meets universal human needs. Its characteristic fruits in human life are seen in every people and culture where it has won followers. The rapid emergence of indigenous leadership in non-Occidental Christian communities in the past twenty-five years bears additional witness to the truth of this generalization. This leadership is appearing among the Negroes of Africa, the high and low castes of India, the Chinese, the Japanese, the Koreans, the Pacific Islanders, and the American Indians as well as among those of European stock. The universality of the appeal and of the effect of Jesus has been demonstrated by experience as has that of no other being who has ever lived on this planet.

It has also been proved by experience that the spread of Christianity is not dependent solely upon the appeal of Jesus to the consciences and aspirations of men. It has been furthered by other factors and forces. Some of these have been contradictory to the spirit of Jesus. Some have been neutral. The support of rulers, often accorded from personal ambition or from purposes of state, the use of armed force, the association with imperialism, the prestige of a higher culture with which Christianity has seemed to be identified, the openings given by commerce, and the migrations of professed Christians—all these have at one time or another assisted in the propagation of the faith. Always where the faith has won wide acceptance it has been through a mixture of motives. What has been termed Christianity never perfectly mirrors Jesus. It is always a compound of Jesus with other elements, some of them repugnant to him.

It has likewise been demonstrated that, in spite of the innate universality of the appeal of Jesus, extraneous factors may prove so adverse that Christianity will be prevented from gaining a foothold or, where once it has been strong, will be entirely eliminated. The blood of the martyrs is not always a guarantee of the continuance of the faith. Wars and persecutions have stamped out Christianity in vast areas. More than once Christianity has yielded ground to another religion. It has suffered especially from Islam. By its nature and the means by which it has been introduced and by which conversions from it have been prevented, Islam has won many times more from Christianity than have been won from it to Christianity. Latterly some of the totalitarian ideologies, notably Russian communism, have reduced the strength of the Christian communities in wide areas.

It must also be said that the spread of Christianity has been due in large part to its association with European peoples. It is that tie which has given the appeal of Jesus the opportunity to demonstrate its universality. So far as can now be seen, had it not been for the expansion of European peoples in the past four and a half centuries Christianity would not have obtained the wide extension which it now enjoys. It is possible, to be sure, that this expansion of Europeans would not have occurred had it not been for the stimulus given by the Christian faith. Certainly that faith was an important cause of that expansion. Yet the expansion was also a cause of the spread of the faith.

When all of these qualifications have been made, the

fact remains of the universality of the appeal of Jesus. Often he arouses, as in the days of his flesh, the most bitter opposition. Indeed, the forces inimical to him attain the greatest dimensions in the areas and among the cultures in which his influence is the most potent. Yet everywhere it is carried, the knowledge of him awakens eager acceptance in some hearts and works striking and characteristic changes. Always that knowledge spreads by contagion. Whatever the other forces with which it is associated, it has invariably taken firm root only when it has been transmitted by souls which have been set on fire by it. The presumption is that an appeal so compelling to some from all races and cultures will continue to be made and to awaken a response.

The persistence and growth of the influence of Jesus seem also to be assured by the proven ability of Christianity to survive the death of cultures with which it has been intimately associated and, after a period of crisis provoked by the collapse of such a culture, not only to win a foothold in the new, succeeding culture but also to make a deeper impress upon it than upon its predecessor. This, indeed, follows as a corollary of the attraction of Jesus in all ages and among all peoples.

As we have seen in the preceding chapters, in each period of the advance of Christianity the basis has been laid for a recession. The very success of Christianity has brought the next major threat. The winning of the religious allegiance of the Roman Empire served to identify Christianity with that realm. When, due to factors entirely outside the Christian faith, that empire and its culture declined, the future of Christianity became very dark. Yet, after a period of recession, Christianity not only won what proved to be the most important of the successor cultures, that of Western Europe of the Middle Ages, but also held a larger share in shaping it than it has had in moulding that of the Græco-Roman world. Indeed, it was the elements which entered Medieval Europe by way of Christianity which were chiefly responsible for making it the channel through which the main stream of civilization flowed on into the future. While it did not become so

nearly exclusively identified with Medieval Western Europe
as it had with the Roman Empire, by A.D. 1400 Christianity had its chief strength in that area. Its success, therefore, again proved a serious menace. When, in the fifteenth
century, Turkish conquests and other factors had limited
Christianity chiefly to Europe, the transition from the
Europe of the Middle Ages to that of the Renaissance and
modern times brought another major threat. Similarly the
close association of the geographic spread of Christianity
in the sixteenth, seventeenth, and eighteenth centuries with
the imperial programmes of Spain and Portugal and with
the absolute monarchies of that period precipitated another
crisis when Spain and Portugal became stagnant and
absolute monarchies were being shaken by revolution. In
the nineteenth century the extension of Christianity both
geographically and into various phases of culture in con-
junction with the expansion of the Occident, private enterprise, *laissez faire*, political democracy, and Anglo-Saxon
Protestantism, made for unparalleled growth and heretofore unequalled influence upon the human race. If, as
now seems to be the case, the features of the nineteenth
century with which the growth of the influence of Jesus
was so closely associated are fading, another recession can
be anticipated. However, since in the past Christianity
has demonstrated its ability to survive the passing of the
order which it has helped to shape and of which it has
seemed to be an inseparable part, it is to be expected that
this again will be the record and that after what may be a
decline Christianity will revive and with increased power
go on to mould, more than before, the human race. Even
if it should lose in some areas where it has once been strong
—perhaps in sections where it has been strongest—this
would be no new phenomenon. That has happened
before. Past experience gives ground for the expectation
that elsewhere, perhaps in some quite unexpected region,
Christianity will encounter an environment in which,
partly because of its own inward vitality, it can achieve a
fresh extension and in which and from which it can
continue its growth.

It must also have been noted, if the earlier chapters have

been perused with care, that during each major recession the preparation has been made for a fresh advance, and, as we hinted at the close of the last paragraph, this has been in quite unexpected quarters. In that disheartening period which followed the fifth century, when Christianity appeared to be passing, geographic gains were being made in Western Europe which formed the basis for most of the next advance. Yet Western Europe was a most unpromising area. In A.D. 500 Christianity was far weaker there than in the Eastern Mediterranean. For centuries, moreover, Western Europe was being overrun by barbarians, most of them pagans. During the decline which accompanied the conquests by the Ottoman Turks and the fading of Medieval European culture, currents of life were appearing which contributed to the later unprecedented revival. Some of the most potent of these currents were not in the south of Europe, where the majority of the new movements which had brought vigour to the Christianity of the Middle Ages originated, but north of that area—in Germany, England, the Low Countries, and Bohemia. Protestantism was chiefly from regions north of the Alps and of Southern France. While much of the revival of Roman Catholicism was through leaders from Italy, it was from the Iberian Peninsula that Ignatius Loyola, the founder of the chief organization of the Roman Catholic Reformation, the Society of Jesus, came, and it was from Spain and Portugal, only recently emerged from the Moslem yoke and where in the seventh and eighth centuries Christianity had suffered some of its worst defeats, that the next chief geographic expansion of Christianity issued. In the period of stagnation and reverse that came in the eighteenth century, revivals were beginning to appear which were to swell into the stream from which issued the major part of the extension of the faith in the nineteenth and twentieth centuries. That extension was not mainly from Roman Catholicism, although the latter had a very large and active share in it, but from Protestantism, whose part in the pre-nineteenth century expansion of Christianity had been relatively minor, and Protestantism spread chiefly not from the traditional centres in which

it had had its inception and in which had arisen its
greatest theologies, but from the British Isles and
the United States. Judging from this record, the
weakening of Christianity in some of the areas in
which it was most potent in the nineteenth century
should not be a cause of dismay. We can expect that a
revival will come from quarters which may now seem to
us unlikely.

In just what regions the next great revival of Christianity will arise we ought not to attempt confidently to
predict. Probably it will be in some area in which there is
a minimum of the control of the Church by the state. That
at least has been a condition of several of the former
awakenings. However, it is not a necessary condition, for
Ignatius Loyola came from a land in which the state had
greatly enhanced its supervision of the Church, and John
Wesley was a priest of a church which seemed hopelessly
subservient to the Crown. The friendship of the absolute
state is not essential, for most of the members of the ruling
classes of eighteenth-century England were scornful of the
early Methodists. Christianity achieved its amazing gains
in the first three centuries against the chronic suspicion
and the recurring active persecution of the Roman authorities. In spite of these seeming exceptions, a certain amount
of freedom from state interference appears a prerequisite
to a renewal of vigorous life in the Church. The great
persecutions of the third and the first part of the fourth
century, if they had persisted, would probably have
wrought far greater damage than they did. For one
reason or another, each was allowed to lag or was brought
decisively to an end by a reversal of policy before it had
continued many years. So, too, at its inception the
Protestant movement was assisted in Germany by the
weakness of the imperial authority and the favour of some
of the local princes. The Jesuits early won royal patronage,
notably that of the King of Portugal. When in the
eighteenth century royal authority turned against them,
they ceased to flourish and were actually driven out of
some kingdoms before their dissolution by the Pope. In spite
of statutory restrictions, Hanoverian England contained

a certain degree of practical religious liberty. The presumption is, therefore, that revival will arise in some region or regions where the state permits a measure of religious liberty or where it is actually friendly to the new movement, even though that favour be from other motives than those of which Jesus could approve.

It may be that in the years just ahead more of the centre of the strength of Christianity will lie in the United States. Certainly in the past few decades this land has been forging to the front in the Christian movement. Here Church and state are separated, but the state is, on the whole, friendly to the Church. Here the proportion of the population who have a formal connection with the Church has been increasing, even since A.D. 1914. While it is affected by the wars of Europe and either as a belligerent or as an active sympathizer with one or another of the contestants has been drawn into each of the general European wars which have been fought within the span of its history, geography has spared the United States the full impact of these wars and the nation has not been so severely impoverished as Europe, nor has its normal life been so badly disrupted. It is enormously wealthy, more so than any other country. Indeed, it is said to have about half the world's wealth. In it democracy survives and, although threatened, is fairly certain of continuing, even though that will undoubtedly be in modified form. In it both Protestantism and Roman Catholicism are strongly represented and both forms of Christianity are drawing from it a mounting share of the funds and personnel for their world-wide enterprises. All of the major Eastern types of Christianity are also present, although as minorities. Unless some cataclysm, now quite unlikely, overwhelms the United States, it seems probable that from it will come in the decades just ahead an increasing proportion of the initiative of the Christian movement. For at least a generation, more and more the influence of Jesus will depend upon the United States for its perpetuation.

In the United States, Christianity may be substantially altered. The falling birth-rate of the older stock may make for a decline in the relative importance of those denominations, largely of Anglo-Saxon origin, which heretofore have set the pace.

It seems clear from past experience that when it comes the renewal of life will have its chief channel through what in the broadest sense is the Church. It may create a new denomination or denominations. Unquestionably it will give rise to new organizations and fellowships. If it is in the Roman Catholic Church, some of these will be orders and congregations. Moreover, it may give birth to movements for the betterment of society which have neither an official nor an unofficial connection with any church. That, at least, has happened repeatedly in the past century and a half. Yet, if the past is any criterion, even the non-ecclesiastical bodies will be deeply indebted to the Church. It is through some form of organized avowedly Christian fellowship of confessed Christians that the impulse given by Jesus is continued from age to age.

It seems probable that, in the age into which we are entering, the Church will be less a community institution and more an organized minority than among European peoples between Constantine and the nineteenth century. Beginning with Constantine and even before Constantine in some areas, such as Armenia, when Christianity became powerful it was usually accepted as the faith of the community and, except for a few intransigent minorities, membership in the Church became coterminous with citizenship. Increasingly in the nineteenth and twentieth centuries a contrary tendency has been evident. In country after country Church and state have been formally separated. This has been due on the one hand to rejection of Christianity and dislike of the Church. On the other it has come from the presence of Christian groups not supported by the state who have resented the exclusive favour of the state for one church, or from the conviction on the part of earnest Christians that the Church should be purified of merely nominal Christians and removed from the control of officials who regard it as an instrument of the state or as a tool of their own private interests. This tendency has been reinforced by the position of the churches in non-Occidental lands. Here, with a few exceptions, usually in some of the smaller islands of the Pacific, Christians have been in the minority. The policy of missionaries, both Roman Catholic and Protestant, has been to place higher standards of instruction and of conformity to Christian morals for admission to church membership than was customary between Constantine and the nineteenth century. In the Roman Catholic Church those adhering to that form of the faith are already knit into a world-wide fellowship under the supervision of a hierarchy culminating in the Pope and more nearly exclusively devoted to the spiritual care of their flock than have been their predecessors for many centuries. Non-Roman Catholic Christians, especially Protestants, are being rapidly brought together into a fellowship which is also world-wide. There seems no likelihood that these two fellowships will coalesce—certainly not at any early date. In general, however, antagonism between the two is less acute than at most former times, perhaps less than in any previous period. The consciousness of a common enemy in the ideologies supported by the totalitarian states has made them lay less stress on differences. What we are seeing, then, is two world-wide Christian fellowships set not primarily against each other but chiefly against the world. In some quarters persecutions have depleted the Christian forces and in a few have driven the remnants underground. This may be the fate which the near future holds in store in still other countries. Yet, as never before, the two fellowships are world-embracing, with a leadership which is increasingly indigenous. The non-Roman Catholic fellowship is still in its early stages but is rapidly coming into being and acquiring self-consciousness. The Roman Catholic fellowship is less hampered by subservience to the state and is more closely integrated under the Papacy than at any previous time. Both are growing in numbers and influence in non-Occidental lands, areas where they have heretofore been weakest.

This position of the Church as a self-conscious minority in two world-wide fellowships, whose strength is increasing most rapidly in the lands in which it has been weakest, augurs well for the future. By its nature Christianity must always be in antagonism to much in the world about it. Yet it must live in that world, bear witness to the Christian Gospel, and seek to permeate the world with its ideals. While it can never hope to bring the world into full conformity to its standards, it must always be striving to do so. Now and again it will make striking progress. This seems to be best accomplished by organized, avowedly Christian fellowships, the churches. These are never entirely free from contamination from the world which they are endeavouring to transform. Yet they are the channels for the undying Christian life. We are living in a time when the human race is being compelled by the machines which it has created to live together. These machines are in part the product of the Christian impulse, although all too often perverted from Christian ends. It is ground for great hope that in this day the Church is finding expression in two world fellowships. Through them it can bring to bear upon the entire race the life of which it is the trustee.

In this world the Church's complete triumph is never assured. In some areas grave reverses will be met. In all areas the Church will be confronted by foes. There is that in human nature which will always be antagonized by Jesus. Yet in human nature there is always that which responds to him. Men everywhere and of every race are both repelled and attracted. Always there will be some who will seek to crucify Jesus. But always, where He is seen, He will win followers. In these followers He will be reincarnated, even though never perfectly. Here and there the crucifiers will kill off His followers. Somewhere, however, followers will survive. From these survivors Jesus will again be carried to the lands from which He has been driven.

In this witnessing Church, always imperfect but always bearing something of the likeness of its Lord and always a channel for its life, is the hope for the continuation of the influence of Jesus in the world. No other religion and none of the modern ideologies has a fellowship which equals the Church in its world-embracing extent and strength. If the present age is one of retreat for Christianity, here, in this day of seeming reverse, is the preparation for the next advance. If, in spite of discouragements, the age is really one of advance, here is the instrument through which the forward sweep of the tide is being manifested.

Always, we need again and again to remind ourselves, the secret of the Church's strength is not organization. Christianity spreads through organizations. Its propagation and perpetuation are aided by many factors, some of them political, some economic, and some intellectual. Yet the real reason for the continuation and expansion of the influence of Jesus is in Jesus Himself. Age after age it is men and women who have been captured by Jesus and have entered a new life through Him who have been the centre of Christian advance, the active agents through whom the faith has gone on. The greatest of early Christians clearly saw this. They declared that Jesus was the expression, in such fashion that men could see it, of the Eternal God Himself, that He was and is the Logos, the Word, through whom God touches Human life, that in Him was life, and that that life is the light of men. Always that light, so they saw, shines in darkness. Yet, they declared, the darkness never puts it out. The experience of nineteen centuries has justified their insight. It is this life and this light which constitute the secret of the power of Christianity and of the Church. It is this life and this light, emanating from the creative heart of the universe and of its very essence, which are the sure hope for the future.